The Art of
Painting Animals on Rocks

The Art of
Painting Animals
on Rocks

Lin Wellford

NORTH LIGHT BOOKS
CINCINNATI, OHIO

ABOUT THE AUTHOR

Lin Wellford comes from a family of artists that includes sculptors, painters and commercial artists. She studied under several instructors before majoring in advertising design at the University of Florida. She has won many awards for her pen-and-ink sketches and watercolors, but since 1978 has concentrated her talents on her "Stone Menagerie."

Wellford's work has received national media attention and continues to be favored by animal lovers and art lovers alike. Each piece is unique because no two stones are ever exactly alike. Every stone creation is signed and finished. Wellford lives in Carroll County, Arkansas with her husband and three daughters.

Other fine North Light Books are available at your local bookstore, art supply store or direct from the publisher.

02 01 00 99 98   13 12 11 10

Library of Congress Cataloging-in-Publication Data

Wellford, Lin
     The art of painting animals on rocks / [by Lin Wellford].
         p.   cm.
     Includes index.
     ISBN 0-89134-572-8
     1. Stone painting. 2. Acrylic painting. 3. Animals in art. I. Title.
TT370.W45   1994
751.4'26—dc20   94-7944
                                                                    CIP

Edited by Jennifer Pfalzgraf
Cover and interior design by Sandy Conopeotis
Cover photography by Pam Monfort

Table *of* Contents

Introduction

Art has undergone countless evolutions since man executed those first paintings on cave walls. Modern artists can choose from a dizzying array of mediums and methods. At the same time, the use of natural, nonmanufactured materials has growing appeal in this age of ecological awareness.

Stone painting represents the perfect marriage of old and new. Technological advances have given us tough, inexpensive acrylic paints and finishes. And weathered rocks can be found all over the world. They are, in fact, so common and plentiful that they are considered by most people to be of little or no value. But for me, collecting stones to paint is like a treasure hunt.

I stumbled onto the art of stone painting by accident after years of doing pen and inks and watercolors. Like many selling artists, I was frustrated by the tidy sums I had tied up in inventory between sales. It seemed the costs of matting, framing and glassing my work were always on the rise.

Shortly after moving to the Ozark Mountains of northwest Arkansas, I picked up a stone the size and shape of a baking potato at a local creek. It looked so much like a rabbit that I felt moved to take it home and give it eyes, ears and a fluffy cotton tail. From the moment I placed tiny white sparkles in the eyes, I was hooked. The transformation from a dull creek rock into a wild rabbit, one that actually seemed to be looking back at me, was almost magical.

Over the past fifteen years I have painted thousands of stone animals. My menagerie has expanded to include creatures as diverse as reptiles, birds and practically anything with a fur coat.

Along the way I've shared my enthusiasm for this unique medium with others. With a little guidance, people of all ages and levels of ability can also experience the magic of "bringing stones to life."

I hope this book will inspire anyone with an artistic bent to give the exciting and fulfilling medium of stone painting a try.

Getting Started

The most pleasing results begin with selecting the right stones for your projects. The best ones are those that have been tumbled and rounded off by water. The logical place to look, therefore, is around moving water. Beaches, creek beds and riverbeds are all sites that offer good pickings. If you are not aware of such places in your area, ask around. Fishermen and other sportsmen can probably offer tips on where to look.

There are a few regions, such as along the Gulf Coast, where suitable stones don't occur naturally. But even in these areas you can locate nurseries and other businesses that sell smooth stones for rock gardens or landscaping purposes. Even landscape stones should cost far less than most traditional art supplies.

In your travels, learn to watch for promising sites. Remember, though, that most state and national parks have rules against taking anything from within their boundaries, including even lowly rocks. Nevertheless, there are abundant roadside creeks and streams where you can gather stones to your heart's content. In all the years I have been collecting them, I have never had a single landowner object.

A few stone types should be avoided. If your area offers sandstones, be aware that some may be in the process of final breakdown. I call this condition "rock rot." Check for it by rubbing your hand lightly over the stone's surface. If loose particles of sand brush away easily, the surface may not accept paint well and the rock should be discarded.

Also consider overall surface smoothness when choosing stones for painting. Some stones are lightly pitted, and you'll find that a bit of texture will add to the appeal of your finished

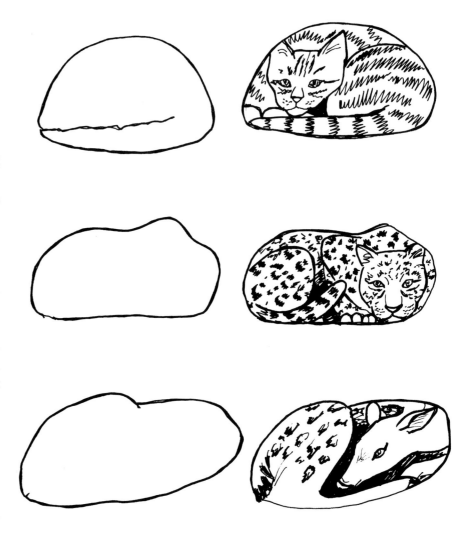

The Art of Painting Animals on Rocks

work. But overly rough or pebbly surfaces may hinder crisp fur lines and other vital details.

As a rule, I reject any stone with a harsh angle or jagged, broken edges. Sometimes a bad side can be used as the base, but generally speaking, beginners should select the smoothest, most uniform rocks available. Odd lumps, creases or cracks don't necessarily make a stone unusable, however. With experience you will learn to see how such defects may actually enhance the realism of your work. For instance, a protruding lump may prove the perfect site for your animal's head, a haunch or even a shoulder blade. A crease or superficial crack might be incorporated to form the tail or define two separate forms as I did with this double squirrel stone. Holes or other small flaws that can't be worked into the design can be camouflaged by filling them in with a bit of 3 in One brand Plastic Wood, a product that dries quickly and can be painted over. I have also used plastic wood to stabilize the base of a "tippy" rock.

Another type of stone I am rarely able to use is the overly flat kind. Such stones simply don't offer enough volume to provide the illusion of contour. Reject any stone that is not at least a couple of inches thick.

The last requirement is that the stone should sit on one more or less flat side. Stones that wobble or fall over don't make good animals. But try turning stones over and around before disqualifying them. Many will have one flatter side that works as the base.

It is a good idea to thoroughly clean your rocks before you begin painting. Use scouring powder or foaming bathroom cleaner and a scrub brush to remove loose debris and caked-on algae, and allow the stone to dry.

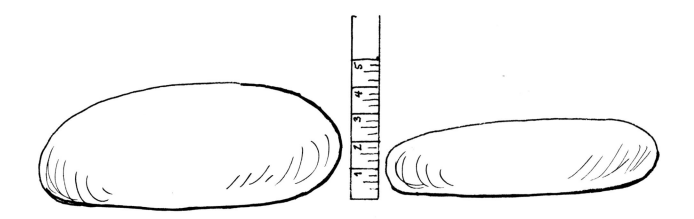

Supplies and Equipment

Most projects in this book can be painted with a limited selection of acrylic paints. You can use the thicker, tubed kind, made specifically for artists, or the liquid type designed primarily for crafters. I prefer the latter as it is closer to the consistancy I need. Both types are widely available at discount stores and craft shops. The small plastic bottles will last a surprisingly long time, but for colors I use frequently, like black and white, I buy the larger-size containers.

My selection of brushes is extensive, but I most often reach for the same three or four favorites. First and foremost is a narrow script liner brush. The ability to make very fine lines and details is vital to all stone painting projects. You can begin with inexpensive craft brushes, but if you find yourself doing a lot of painting, consider investing a little more in a good sable brush. It will far outlast most synthetic bristles. My current favorite is a Loew-Cornell #1, stock number 8050, but I'm always on the lookout for narrow bristle brushes that hold a fine point through repeated use.

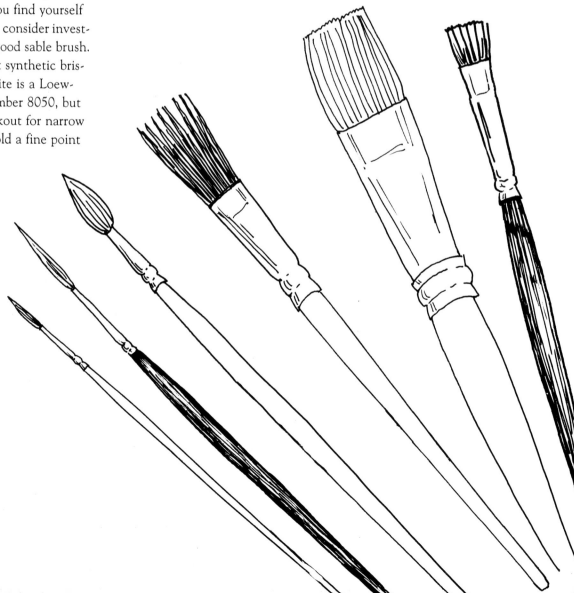

You will also need a wide, flat brush for covering large areas quickly, a medium, round-bristled brush, like a Robert Simmons #5, and a similar-sized brush with a squared off tip sometimes called a "scrubber." If you have any old, worn brushes whose bristles have separated don't throw them out. These are great for making multiple fur lines in a hurry.

A pie pan or old dinner plate makes an acceptable palette, along with a plastic cup for rinsing off brushes.

To set up a work place you'll need nothing more than a roomy table with good overhead illumination. Cover your work space with enough newspaper to protect the tabletop from abrasion. This newspaper underlay will also prove indispensible for wiping excess water from your brushes and for checking paint consistency. I always recycle my newspapers one more time by using them to wrap finished pieces for shipping.

A low turntable of some kind makes work on heavier stones less awkward.

The only other requirements are a good supply of pencils, chalk, a measuring tape, and a bit of imagination.

If you enjoy doing the projects in this book, I recommend you begin building a library of photographs of various animals. Even though I paint many animals over and over, I find that good photographs are an inspiration and help keep my work fresh.

A final note: These instructions are designed to help creative people get started in an exciting new medium. But remember that all artists bring their own unique vision, talent and style to any work they do. There is no "right" or "wrong" way to paint stones or

anything else. What matters is pleasing yourself. My hope is that these projects will serve as a "jumping-off place" from which you can develop a style as unique and individual as you are.

What You'll Need

- acrylic paints
- narrow script liner brush
- wide, flat brush
- medium, round-bristled brush
- "scrubber" brush with squared-off tip
- palette
- cup for rinsing brushes

The Art of Painting Animals on Rocks

How to Paint a
Ladybug

The simple design and bold colors make this ladybug an ideal first stone to paint.

As with every project in this book, success depends on selecting the right rock to begin with. A potential ladybug stone might be as small as a bottle cap or as big as a dinner plate, but your best bet is to look for a smooth stone between 2″ and 4″ in diameter. If your rock is too large your "bug" risks losing the appeal of being cute. On the other hand, a stone smaller than 2″ across will require far more skill and concentration.

The stone you choose may be perfectly round or slightly oval in shape so long as it is symmetrical. The best

A perfect ladybug stone.

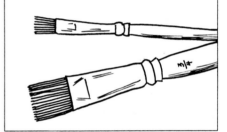

What You'll Need

- black, red (or other bright color of your choice), white and blue acrylic paints
- a 1″-wide brush
- a medium, tapered brush
- a narrow script liner brush
- a pencil
- sheet of paper (optional)
- scissors
- a note card

bugs are rounded like a dome on top, but your stone may be only slightly curved on top and still work. The bottom side, however, must be fairly flat.

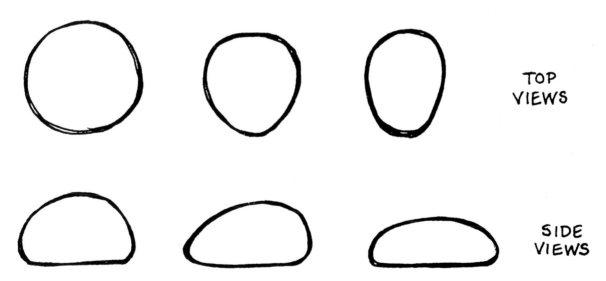

TOP VIEWS

SIDE VIEWS

Ladybug rocks can be round, oval or tear-shaped.

1 Layout.

When you have found a promising stone, scrub and let it dry. Then sketch the wings on freehand as shown. Or, if you prefer, use the template method to lay out the wings.

Wing pattern.

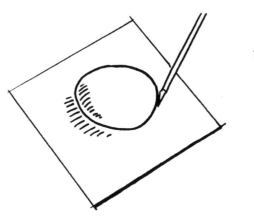

1. Set your stone on a piece of paper and carefully trace all the way around the bottom with a pencil.

2. Cut out the circle or oval you just traced.

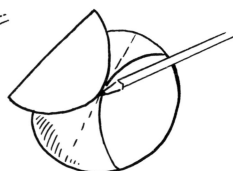

3. Fold it in half. The curving side will serve as the plate for the ladybug's wings.

4. With a pencil and ruler or other straightedge, draw a line down the exact center of your stone.

5. Place the curved edge of your template so it covers half of the stone. Now carefully trace around the curved edge of your template. Flip the pattern over and reposition to make a matching curved line on the opposite side.

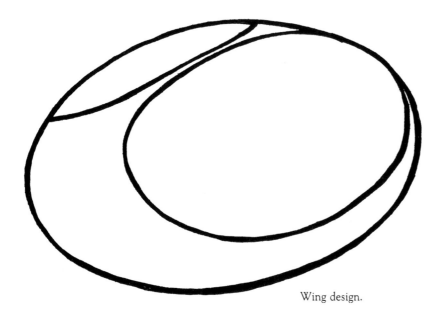

Wing design.

Your stone should be divided into three sections: two equal wings and a slightly smaller head area, leaving only a slight triangle showing at the tail end where the wings curve in opposite directions. Round out your wing shapes into ovals. If your first attempt isn't satisfactory, simply scrub away the pencil marks and try again.

2 Painting the Black Areas.

Pour a small puddle of black acrylic paint into your painting dish. If you're using craft paint you probably won't need to add water. With tube paint, however, you may need to experiment with water to obtain the right consistency. The paint should be loose enough to apply easily, but retain enough body for solid coverage. If your paint is runny or if the stone shows through when dry, your paint was too thin and may require a second coat. If, on the other hand, your brush drags dryly over the stone and coverage is rough and broken, try moistening your paint by adding drops of water sparingly.

Use black to cover every part of the stone except the oval wings and the bottom of the stone. You can use a larger brush for most areas, but switch to your smallest brush to paint the line where the two wings come together on top. This line should not be more than ⅛" wide. Allow the black paint to dry thoroughly before you go on to the next step.

Cover every part of the stone except the wings.

Turn your stone to paint around the wings.

3 Adding Wing Color.

Have you decided what color you want your bug to be? Red, yellow and orange are all good choices, but lighter colors may need several coats for complete coverage. Paint around the edges of the wings, keeping your strokes steady. If you need more than one coat, let the paint dry between applications.

Turn your stone around as you paint to insure that your wings are colored in all the way around. If you accidently paint over the black undercoat at any point, don't panic. Simply allow the area to dry, then go over it with a little more black paint to repair the place.

Red, yellow and orange are good choices for wing colors.

How to Paint a Ladybug

Suggested spot designs.

4 Painting the Spots.

How many decorative spots you paint and where they go is up to you. You may only want a couple of large spots on each side, or you may decide to scatter smaller ones about. However many you choose to paint, be sure to space them uniformly so they don't touch or overlap. Both wings should match. Use a pencil to sketch spots on the dried wing areas. Remember that sketch marks can be painted over at any point and redone until you are satisfied.

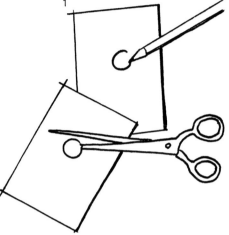

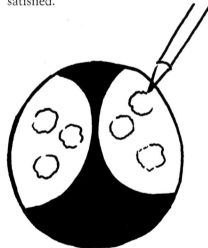

You can sketch the spots on freehand with a pencil.

If you don't feel you can paint a round spot freehand or if you want all the spots exactly the same size, try making a stencil. (1) Trace a circle of the desired size on a note card or other stiff material. (2) Cut out the center. (3) Line the hole up over one of the spots you sketched onto your stone. Press firmly around the edges of the stencil to hold it in place and use your medium brush to dab on just enough

black paint to fill in the circle. Carefully lift the card straight up to avoid smearing. Allow each spot to dry before going on to the next. To speed things up, switch to the other wing and work there while waiting. (4) After you have completed your pattern of spots and let them dry, you may need to go around some of them with the wing color and smallest brush to smooth rough edges.

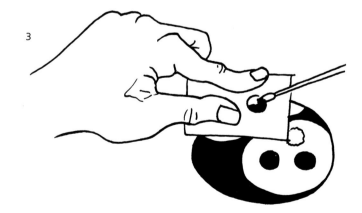

5 The Face.

Your bug's personality will be determined by the expression she wears. I prefer a happy look, but there are many other choices.

Whether you use one of my expression designs or make up your own, take extra care when painting your bug's features. Use a small brush and be sure the paint is thick enough to show up against the black background of the face. You may have to go over the features more than once to make them stand out clearly. If you aren't happy with your first attempt, you can always paint out what you don't like and try again.

To protect your bug and make the colors look brighter, you may wish to seal the surface. Use spray-on polyurethane or wipe on an acrylic finish such as Future floor polish with a lint-free cloth.

After you've painted a ladybug or two, you may feel like really going buggy! Bugs come in an amazing array of shapes and colors. Books about insects are a great place to get ideas for other kinds of bugs to try painting. Or use your imagination to come up with your own make-believe bugs.

Buggy expressions.

Use thick white paint for the eyeballs.

Adding antennae.

An array of colorful bugs.

How to Paint a Ladybug

The Art of Painting Animals on Rocks

How to Paint a
Snake

These "rocky reptiles" are only a little more involved than ladybugs and make another excellent project for beginning stone painters. My stone coral snake has an interesting pattern of variegated bands that is colorful yet still relatively simple to paint.

The best snake stones are either round or oval, 6″ to 7″ in diameter and 2″ or 3″ thick at their center. As with all stone projects, begin by scrubbing your stone and allowing it to dry.

A perfect snake rock.

Top Views

Side Views

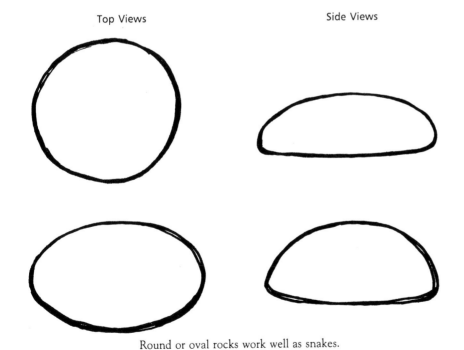

Round or oval rocks work well as snakes.

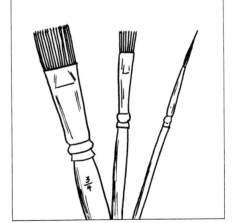

What You'll Need

- acrylic paints in black, yellow, red and white
- large, medium and narrow brushes
- a pencil

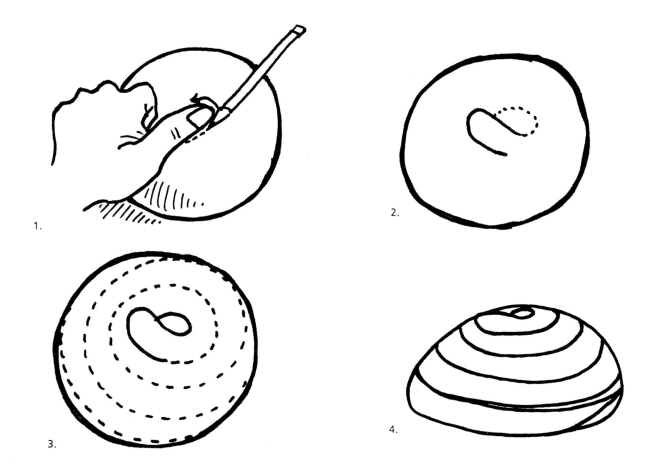

1.

2.

3.

4.

1 Layout.

Sketch an elongated head in the middle of the stone. To get the proper proportions, try tracing around the first joint of your thumb (if your thumb is very small, ask to "borrow" someone else's thumb).

Next rotate the stone so the head points to your left. (Not all snakes have to face left, but it will be easier to follow these instructions if your first one does.) Place your pencil on the upper line of the head and extend that line so it curves up and loops back around

to meet at the middle of the head. This loop forms the center of your snake's coils.

Now place your pencil at the end of the lower head line and begin to form the coils. Try to keep all the coils around the same width (1″ or so).

As you near the bottom edge of your stone, narrow the width until you have nearly run out of room. At that point, allow the upper and lower lines to gradually come together to form the tip of the tail.

That completes your basic layout. Now you can fine-tune some of the details. Coral snakes have blunt, oval-shaped heads. If you choose to do a different kind of snake at some point, you may want to modify the shape of the head to reflect variations between species.

The Art of Painting Animals on Rocks

Snake head varieties.

2 Painting the Coils.

With black paint and a medium-sized brush, outline the coils and fill in the area that forms the center between your snake's coils. Also darken the spaces above and below where the tail tapers off. Set your stone down and turn it, checking that no bare stone shows below your bottommost coil.

Painting the coil lines.

Taper the tip of the tail.

3 Laying Out the Rings.

Laying out the pattern is easy.

Coral snakes have a black snout followed by a fairly wide yellow band covering the remainder of the head. A slightly wider black band falls at the neck. At this point begin a repeating pattern of wide red bands with alternating, equally wide black bands sandwiched between skinny yellow bands. Continue this to where the tail tapers to a point. There the pattern reverts to black-yellow-black-yellow in diminishing bands to the tip. As you sketch in the pattern for these bands, curve your lines to create the illusion that your coils are rounded, not flat.

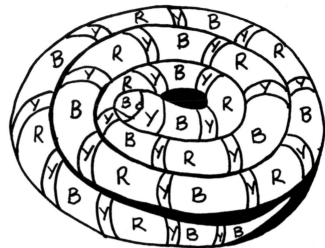

Use letters to color code your ring patterns.

4 Painting the Bands.

Paint the yellow areas first. Use a medium-sized brush and begin with the band at the head. It will probably take two coats to get a solid, vivid color. Next switch to red and fill in the area right behind the first yellow band. Leave the next wide band blank. From there on, color in every other wide band with red. Note that the joints between color bands do not have to be perfectly even or clean. In fact, a deliberate, slightly jagged effect where the colors meet creates more realism.

When the red areas have dried, complete the pattern by filling in the black bands.

Sketching the bands.

Yellow bands.

Red bands.

Black bands.

The Art of Painting Animals on Rocks

5 Finishing Touches.

After the black areas have dried, paint in a small red eye circle with your narrowest brush. The eye should be placed in the black area of the snout about ⅛" from the beginning of the first yellow band. Using the same fine brush, define individual coils by mixing a drop of red paint with just enough black to get a deep maroon color. Stroke three or four thin, closely spaced horizontal lines along the bottom half of every red band. These brush lines need not be perfectly uniform. Your snake will actually look more realistic if they are somewhat uneven and random.

Highlight the red coils with maroon strokes.

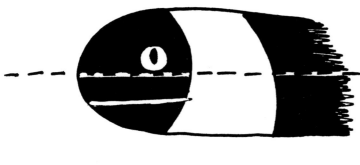

The bottom of the eye should rest on the imaginary midline of the head.

Heighten your snake's realism with horizontal lines along the bottom of each coil.

Rinse your brush well and switch to a light gray by mixing small amounts of black and white. Use this color to redefine any area where two black portions of successive coils are touching. Also outline around the tip of the snout, and paint in a mouth line as shown. Then, as you did previously with the maroon, use this gray to highlight the top and bottom of each black band. These strokes will suggest light reflected off the curving coils. Remember to highlight the tip of the tail so that it, too, will stand out. Finally, use a tiny dot of pure white to create a sparkle of light in your snake's eye.

When the paint has dried, apply liquid or spray finish to bring the colors out more vividly. Don't forget to sign your finished artwork!

Separate adjacent black coils with thin gray lines.

Highlight black coils with gray.

The Art of Painting Animals on Rocks

Once you've mastered the basics, there are endless varieties of snakes that are fun to paint. And if these more realistic-looking snakes give you the willies, try painting a fantasy serpent instead. Use the wildest color schemes you can imagine, and dream up your own patterns to create fun, fanciful decorative pieces.

A striking likeness of a coral snake.

Fantasy serpents.

The Art of Painting Animals on Rocks

How to Paint a
Stone Turtle

Turtles have a reputation for being pokey little critters, but with these step-by-step directions you can turn a stone into a turtle with surprising speed.

Look for a round, oval or even teardrop-shaped rock. The best turtle stones are slightly larger than ladybugs, somewhere between 4″ to 5″ across. Look for a symmetrical stone that's flat on the bottom and dome-shaped on top.

Prepare your stone for painting by scrubbing well and letting it dry.

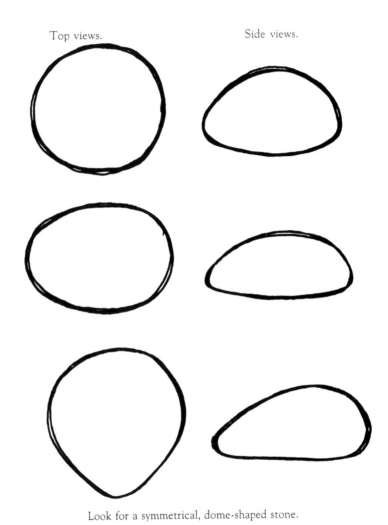

Top views.   Side views.

Look for a symmetrical, dome-shaped stone.

A good turtle rock.

What You'll Need

- black, green, yellow, red and brown (or blue) acrylic paints
- large, medium and narrow brushes
- a pencil

1 Layout.

To lay out the basic design, begin with the head. If you've chosen a teardrop-shaped stone, the head should go where the point protrudes. With a round or oval stone you'll need to decide for yourself which site is best for the head. To achieve proper proportion, the oval head shape on a 4″ stone, should be approximately 1½″ across by about 1″ wide. The turtle's chin should rest at the midline of the stone's width. Once you've drawn the head, begin sketching in the shell. Start directly behind the head and follow the contour in a gentle curve descending down to the midline of the stone all the way around.

When completed, this line should form the circular (or, if you have an oval rock, oval) shape of the upper shell, with an indentation around the head. Turn the stone so the head is facing you and sketch in a squarish segment to represent the connection between the top and bottom shell on both sides.

To form the front legs, angle small oval shapes slanting diagonally from the midline in toward the head. Add four pointy toes to each foot. Below and between the front feet draw a straight horizontal line to indicate the bottom of the shell. Extend this line all the way around the bottom edge of the stone. At the back end make the tail by drawing a small, elongated triangle extending down from the upper shell line. The tail will look more realistic if you curve it slightly to one side. Angle the back legs out from the upper shell at either side of the tail. This completes the basic layout.

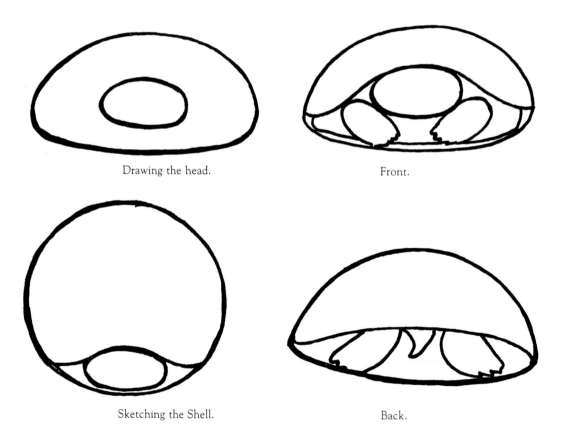

Drawing the head.

Front.

Sketching the Shell.

Back.

The Art of Painting Animals on Rocks

2 Creating Contours.

Use black paint and your small brush to give the stone the illusion of having contours. Outline around the head oval, front legs, tail, and back legs, then fill in any remaining areas between the top and bottom shells all the way around. Do not paint over the connecting side segments. Be sure the line around the top of the head is distinct so the head stands out. Allow the paint to dry.

Side view of turtle layout.

Outline the head and legs in black.

3 Adding a Base Color.

Mix enough shell color to cover all remaining surface areas. I mix a medium green with just enough brown to create a subtle, understated olive color. You may prefer to use straight green, or to mix green and blue for a deep turquoise. The darker the basic shell color is, the more contrast you'll have when you paint in the details later. You can use your largest brush to fill in the top shell fast, but for better control, use your small or medium brush to color in the the head, legs and tail. Also paint the connecting segments between the top and bottom shell at this time. Allow the green to dry.

4 The Shell Pattern.

When the stone is thoroughly dry, use a pencil to lay out the shell pattern. First sketch a parallel border along the inside of the upper shell. The border should not be more than ½" wide.

Now divide the shell into sections, starting with one directly above the head. You should end up with six, more or less equal, four-sided segments around the outside with one six-sided, segment in the center. The outer segments should taper inward. If you aren't happy with your first attempt, mix some matching green paint, cover over your marks and try again.

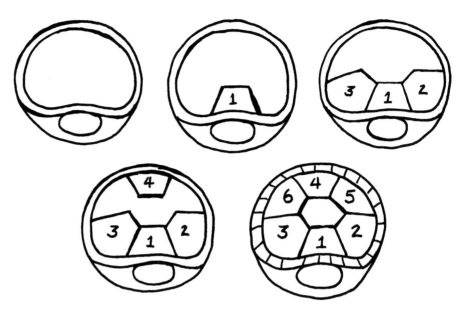

Drawing in the shell segments.

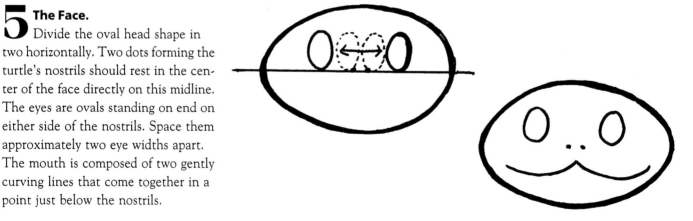

Make a border along the edge of the top shell.

Mistakes can always be painted over and re-drawn.

5 The Face.

Divide the oval head shape in two horizontally. Two dots forming the turtle's nostrils should rest in the center of the face directly on this midline. The eyes are ovals standing on end on either side of the nostrils. Space them approximately two eye widths apart. The mouth is composed of two gently curving lines that come together in a point just below the nostrils.

The Art of Painting Animals on Rocks

6 Adding Details.

Now you're ready to paint details. Use your smallest brush and bright yellow paint to trace all the pencil marks on the shell. Start with the inside and outside borders of the shell, then do the lines for each individual shell segment. It may take more than one coat for the lines to stand out sharply against the green background. Divide the outside border of the shell into small rectangular segments by painting short, vertical lines at intervals all the way around. Allow the paint to dry between coats for best results.

Moving to the head, duplicate the markings around the eyes along the bottom of the mouth and down the chin as shown in the illustration. Also paint the edge of the bottom shell with yellow where it shows between the front feet and back feet. Outline the edges of the connecting side segments also. I like to paint broken or dotted yellow lines down the front legs for added visual interest. While these details dry, mix a small amount of red with yellow paint to get a deep orange. Use this to fill in the eye ovals. You may also use this orange paint to punch up the yellow lines of your shell segments here and there. Use this orange also to highlight the dots on the legs. These touches are not vital, but they will enhance the realism of your turtle.

Outline the shell segments with a bright color.

Add character and vibrancy with bright yellow markings.

7 Finishing Touches.

When the orange eyes are dry, paint a small black iris in the center of each one. At the same time, carefully outline the eyes with black to make them stand out clearly. Create bulging eye sockets by echoing the shape of the eyes in black as shown.

Clean your brush well and mix a combination of green and yellow to get a light green. Use this color to create the geometric pattern on each segment of the turtle's shell. The simplest design resembles a squared-off capital G. If you're good at doing fine lines, you can make sets of nesting squares instead. Finish by placing a tiny dot of pure white at the edge of the iris in each eye to give your turtle the "sparkle of life." Sign the bottom and apply a coat of finish to heighten the colors.

Look for photos in magazines or books for more ideas of other varieties of turtles. Box turtles are basically brown but some have wonderful shell patterns.

Outline the orange eyes in black.

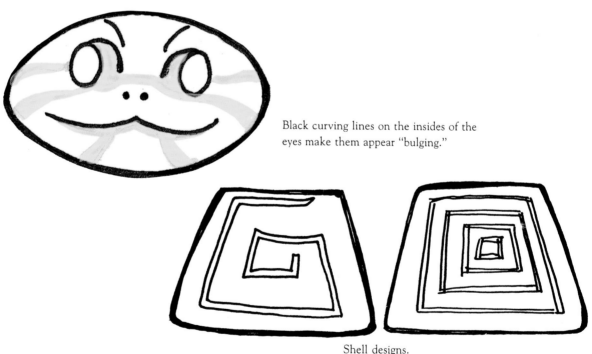

Black curving lines on the insides of the eyes make them appear "bulging."

Shell designs.

The Art of Painting Animals on Rocks

Bright geometric patterns mimic real-life turtle shells.

A finished turtle —
ready for a swim.

27

The Art of Painting Animals on Rocks

How to Paint a
Rock Rabbit

When you're ready to tackle a more detailed project, this wild rabbit is a good place to start. Select a smooth stone similar in shape to a large baking potato. The stone should have a flat bottom so it will sit without rolling over.

While the ideal rabbit rock is oval as shown in view A, there are many variations that will also work. Your stone may be taller and narrower (B), it may have a blunt, somewhat squared shape, (C) or taper off slightly at one end (D). The most important features are a flat bottom for stability and overall symmetry of shape.

Once you find a promising stone, prepare the surface with a good scrubbing and allow to dry. Beginners will find it easier to paint on a stone with a smooth or fine-grained surface. It's much more difficult to achieve the kind of detail you'll want on a rough or pitted surface.

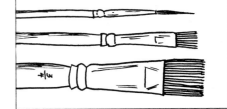

What You'll Need

- acrylic paints in black, white, gold, red and burnt sienna
- large, medium and narrow brushes
- a pencil or piece of chalk

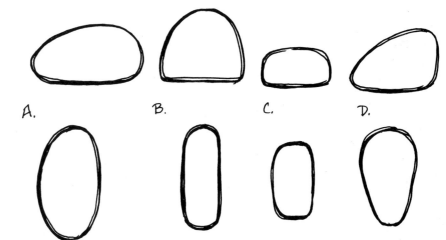

Side views.

A.   B.   C.   D.

Top views.

A variety of stone sizes and shapes will work as painted rabbits.

A perfect rabbit rock.

1 Layout.

Using your largest brush, cover all but the very bottom of your stone with a coat of black paint. If the stone dries with a grayish cast, apply a second, heavier coat. When the paint is dry you can begin sketching in basic shapes. Imagine your stone is divided into thirds (view A). The first third encompasses the jowl area, and the back third is the haunch area. With a sharpened pencil or white chalk, lightly sketch in these guidelines. Sketch curving jowl lines on both sides of the head end, and check from the top to be sure both jowls are about the same. At the top of the stone (view B) these two lines meet to form the forehead. The ears begin at the top of the forehead, extending backward toward the middle of the stone (view B).

Now move to the face (view C). Imagine the front of your stone is divided into quarters. The bottoms of the eyes will rest on a bisecting horizontal line. Eyes that are too large in proportion to the stone will give your bunny a "cartoon" look, so keep them small. Allow a minimum of one and one-half eye widths between them. Check for symmetry by lining up a pencil with the bottom of the eye circles.

If you aren't satisfied with your guidelines at any point, simply dab them away with a damp rag or go over them with more black paint and try again.

Next, center a nose triangle along the vertical bisecting line. It shouldn't be much wider across the top than one of the eyes. Turn your stone around and add an oval-shaped tail to the rear end (view D). Tuck two sets of paws along the bottom edge of either side. Now you're ready to begin painting.

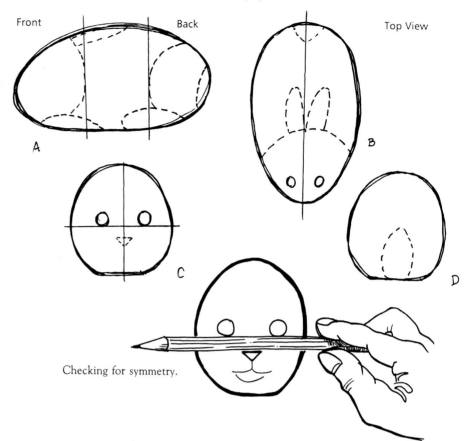

Checking for symmetry.

Paws should be easily visible but not too big.

2 White Contrasts.

Fill in the paws and tail areas with white, using enough paint for solid coverage.

The paws and tail look fluffier if you feather your strokes outward along the edges. Next switch to a smaller brush to paint in two short white lines along the bottom angles of the nose. Outline the basic shape of the ears. Paint a second, parallel line inside the upper edge of each ear to indicate a flap.

Add a line to the inside of each ear to make a flap.

The Art of Painting Animals on Rocks

3 Eyelashes.

Still using white paint and your small brush, stroke in a series of delicate "eyelash" lines. Begin at the outside upper corner of each eye and stroke in a long, curved line extending nearly to the base of the ear. Add more lashes, shortening them as you work toward the inside of each eye. Make a fringe of shorter, curving lashes along the bottom edges of both eyes. Leave an outline of black between these lash lines and the eye circle.

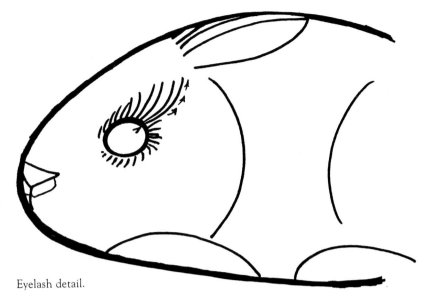

Eyelash detail.

Painting the eyes step-by-step.

4 Eye and Ear Color.

Fill in both eye circles with burnt sienna. Keep the eyes neat and round. If they look uneven, or if you accidently paint over the eyelash lines, let your brown paint dry, then use black to recircle and redefine the eyes later. Add a touch of golden yellow paint to the sienna on your palette and blend to get a lighter shade of brown. With this color form a half-circle inside the bottom portion of each eye. This will give the eyes a more lifelike depth. When the eyes are dry, use black paint to make two oval irises. They should touch the top of each eye circle.

Work on the ears next. Clean your brush well and mix small amounts of red with white until you have a medium shade of pink. Add just enough gold to soften it to a pale fleshtone. Use this color to fill in the insides of the ears, not quite meeting the white outlines you painted earlier. Leave the ear flap unpainted for now. Add burnt sienna to darken the fleshtone on your palette. Use this new color to create a shadowed effect along the upper edges of the ears just below the ear flaps.

Shading the insides of the ears.

5 Fur Lines.

You're now ready to paint in the fur lines that will give your rabbit its soft, realistic look. Fur lines should be as thin and delicate as possible. Dilute the paint enough to flow on easily but not to the point of transparency. You'll want your fur lines to dry crisp and clear. Begin the fur by making a series of short, perpendicular strokes following the curved line of the jowl. Refer to the directional guide at right for guidance in placing your strokes.

Do a second row of longer strokes just inside the first set. Allow each line to taper into a point by easing the pressure on the brush as you lift. Create a shingled effect, allowing your rows to overlap slightly. Vary the direction and size of your strokes for realism.

Three or four sets of overlapping fur lines should bring you close to the bottom eyelashes. Be sure to stop before reaching these lash lines so that some dark contrast remains around the eye areas. Repeat the process with the other jowl, then move on to the haunches.

Follow the arrows on this guide for realistic fur patches.

Fill in the haunch with rows of strokes that angle out like spokes on a wheel. Start on the outside and work toward the center of each haunch. Overlap your strokes to create a shingled effect.

Next, move to your rabbit's back. Start between the ears, leaving a narrow area of black paint surrounding the ears for contrast. Work back toward the tail, varying the length and angle of your strokes. You may indicate

shoulders by allowing your strokes to form an M-shaped row behind the head. Skip a space and start a fresh row of fur farther back. Leave several other similar spaces showing as you continue to work toward the back of the stone. Stop just short of the tail. Allow your lines to dwindle in number as you move down the body so that much of the bottom remains plain black above the paws.

Feather the jowl line with tiny short strokes.

Fill in the haunch with strokes that angle out like spokes in a wheel.

The Art of Painting Animals on Rocks

Remember to leave open spaces around the ears and other features.

Tiny fur lines soften the ears.

6 Facial Features.

The nose, muzzle and forehead are next. Darken a little deep pink paint with a bit of burnt sienna. Fill in the center of the nose triangle, leaving an outline of black surrounding it.

Clean your brush and switch to white paint. Make a series of tiny, splinter-sized fur strokes along the outsides of the ears to make them softer and more natural looking. Scatter some longer whisker lines in the pink part of each ear.

The forehead fur begins just above the nose and fans upward and outward in uneven, shingled rows. Stop before you reach the base of the ears and make one final row of dense, short lines along the top of the head. Leave an area of black showing between these lines and the base of the ears for contrast.

Facial features.

You may find it easier to paint the forehead fur by holding your stone upside down.

Muzzle detail.

Whisker detail.

7 Finishing Touches.

Define the muzzle area below the nose by stroking in two matching circular shapes of tiny fur lines on either side. Leave a narrow line of dark paint between each muzzle circle. Stroke in a semicircle of white fur for the chin beneath the muzzle, also leaving a narrow line of black between the chin and muzzle. These dark lines form the mouth in an anchor shape. Go over the mouth lines with black if necessary.

Switch to gold paint and highlight the outside edges of the muzzle with more tiny fur lines. Also scatter gold fur lines among the white fur elsewhere on your rabbit. These will add realism to the fur. Take the time to put a few gold furs in every area of the bunny's coat, including the forehead. Add a touch of sienna to the gold and stroke this color back along the ear flaps, but leave plenty of black showing.

With more sienna, create a fan-shaped set of lines just above the nose triangle and encircling the outside edges of the muzzle. Add a touch of

black to the sienna and use this darker shade to dot the muzzle with whisker follicles.

Rinse out your brush and carefully mix white paint with just enough water so it will flow in distinct lines. Draw out three or four long, curving whiskers from each side of the muzzle. Finally, dab a dot of white paint in the iris of each eye. This sparkle will make your bunny come alive. Be sure to

place the dot in the same spot in both eyes or your bunny may appear cross- or goggle-eyed.

Look your rabbit over from every angle. Do you have enough fur lines for a soft, fuzzy look? If not, add a few. If some of your fur lines have run together to form a distracting blotch, use a hairline stroke of black to redefine them. You may want to bring out the whiskers by carefully underlining them

A completed rock rabbit.

A "litter" of new bunnies.

with a narrow, parallel line of black paint.

When you're satisfied, turn the stone over to sign and date with a marker or laundry pen. A light application of spray-on polyurethane seals and brings out the rich colors of your piece.

If you display your stone artwork on a countertop or table, gluing a circle of dark felt around the bottom prevents scratching. Or try displaying your bunny in a basket or tucked in among your potted houseplants. Rock rabbits make great gifts at Easter or anytime. Put them to work as paperweights or doorstops. Or group them in "litters" for an absolutely irresistible centerpiece.

Display your rock rabbits in baskets or nestle them in the bases of houseplants.

The Art of Painting Animals on Rocks

How to Paint a
Calico Kitten

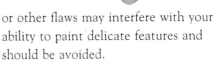

W ith their wide, innocent eyes and furry-looking, compactly curled little bodies, stone kittens are nearly as irresistible as the real thing. People can't resist picking them up or stroking them just to see what they're made of.

Stone kittens can be rendered in an incredible variety of colors and breeds. They make ideal gifts. This project is designed especially for painters with a knack for creating delicate fur lines. But the pattern of calico patches should allow even those with moderate skills to achieve results they can be proud of.

A number of stone shapes are suitable. The most common choice is an oval stone, but round ones work well,

too. A plump, kidney-shaped stone is practically made to order if you happen to find one. Kittens can also be done in a more upright, crouching position, but for this project, let's concentrate on the curled pose. Look for a stone that is between 5" and 7" long and neither too flat (less than 2" high) nor so rounded as to resemble a ball.

Choose a stone with a smooth surface. Occasionally a crack or other flaw can be incorporated into the overall design, like a crack that corresponds to where the tail might curve around the stone. An odd bump at one end could be the perfect place for a head. I enjoy finding stones with unusual features that work in harmony with the piece. Conversely, any cracks, severe pitting

A perfect kitten rock should fit in the palm of your hand.

or other flaws may interfere with your ability to paint delicate features and should be avoided.

Proper proportion is a major consideration in how well your stone kitten will turn out. Take time and care with your basic layout and you will be rewarded with a better end result.

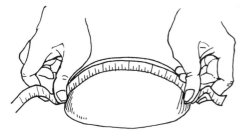

Measure your stone's width
across the top.

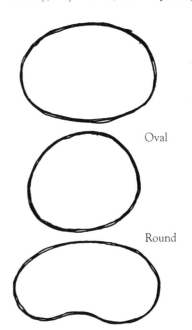

Oval

Round

Kidney-Shaped

What You'll Need

- black, white, burnt sienna, gold, red and medium green acrylic paints
- large and medium brushes
- a good script liner brush
- a pencil
- measuring tape (optional)

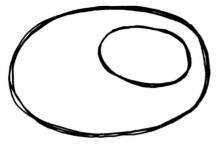

Head too small

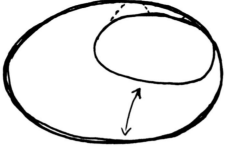

Head too far back

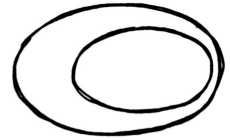

Head too large.

1 Head Placement.

When your stone is scrubbed and dry, set it on a flat surface and decide on the best place for the head. The stone should sit solidly on one flat side. To give you an idea of proportion, on my 6″ stone (measured lengthwise) the kitten's head spans approximately 3″ from cheek to cheek.

But how do you decide where to put the head in the first place? Keep in mind the ears will extend an inch or more above the basic oval shape of the head, so set the head low enough to keep the ears from disappearing around the curved edge of the stone. Also, leave room beneath the head for the front paws to show. A good rule of thumb is to locate the head so it is as far over to one side as the contours of the rock will allow, and just high enough to leave room for the paws. Sketch in the oval head shape, which will be roughly half the length of the stone.

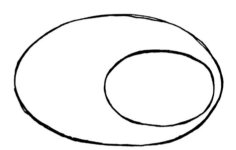

Head in proper proportion and location.

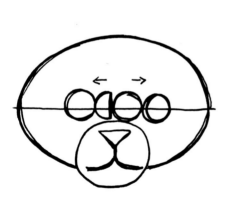

Eyes should be 1½ eye widths apart.

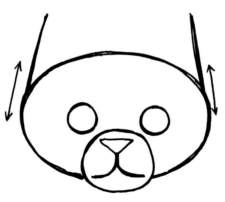

Extending the ear lines.

Ear triangles should be about 1″ high.

2 Facial Features.

Form the muzzle by drawing a circle approximately 1″ across in the bottom half of the face oval. Allow the lower third of the circle to dip below the bottom of the oval. At the top of the muzzle, sketch in a small triangle for the nose. Then add lines for the mouth as shown.

To determine eye placement, bisect the head horizontally. The eye circles will fall at this midline. Begin the eyes about ½″ in from the outer face edge on either side. Between the two eyes leave a space equivalent to one and one-half eye widths.

Finally, extend a line up from each side of the face to form the outside edge of each ear. Kitten ears can vary in size depending on breed and age, but 1″ long is a safe choice. The inside ear edge angles back down to the head, creating a triangular shape. The space between the two ears should equal the width of one ear at its base.

3 Haunches, Paws and Tail Layout.

With the head in place it's fairly simple to complete the layout. The kitten's haunch is also an oval, at an angle to the head shape. Leave at least ¼" between the inside edge of the haunch and the curve of the face oval.

Curve the tail up from below and behind the haunch until the tip reaches almost to the face edge. Again, leave at least ¼" between the two features. By allowing the tip of the tail to curl slightly you'll help distinguish it from the front paw. The paws are formed from two long, narrow ovals below the kitten's chin. Situate them so the space between the paws is not directly in line with the chin but rather slightly off-center.

When you are satisfied with your sketch, darken the features with black paint and medium-sized brush. Also blacken the areas around the front paws, tail and between head and haunch all the way up to the tip of the ear. With your smaller brush, trace the outlines for the eyes. Try to make the outside edges neatly rounded and the same size on both eyes.

Main features can be simplified into basic shapes.

Outline the facial features in black.

4 The Calico Pattern.

While calico kittens come in every imaginable combination of colors and patches, I've arranged the patches in this pattern to show off the kitten's features. Begin by sketching a blaze between and above the eyes that covers both sides of the cheeks and the whole muzzle. Next draw in a raggedy "collar" between the ears, and sketch another longer band behind that one. The pattern on the haunch is divided into three parts like an inverted Y. Also mark off the last inch of the tail and a similar-sized half-circle patch on the tail just below the haunch. On the back side of the stone, make two more wide, curving bands stretching from the haunch to the other side of the stone.

Front.

Back.

5 Blocking in Patches.
Use a clean, medium brush and white paint to block in the white areas as shown. These include the blaze and lower half of the head. Be careful not to go over your guidelines as you paint around the nose and mouth. Next, fill in the front paws and the collar-shaped patch behind the ears as well as the middle haunch section and all of the tail except for the tip and the half-circle patch. Finally, skip over the band directly behind the "collar" and paint in the next one.

Clean your brush and switch to gold paint. Gold patches appear on the side of the head nearest the haunch, the section of the haunch facing the head, the tip and half-circle patch on the tail, and the lowest band on the kitten's backside. Switch to your smallest brush and carefully paint a slender gold line around the kitten's outside ear. Don't cover the black outline around the ear. You'll need this to make the ear stand out.

Complete your base coat by filling in any remaining areas with black (with the exception of the eyes, nose and ears).

White patches.

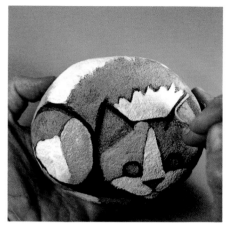
Gold patches.

Black patches.

6 Nose and Ears.
For the insides of the ears, mix two or more drops of white paint with one drop of red to get a deep pink. Use this color with your smallest brush to fill in the triangle nose. Go over the mouth guidelines with this color as well. Now add just enough gold to soften the pink to a fleshtone. Use this color to fill in the triangle shape of the ears.

Mix a deep pink for the nose.

Soften the pink to a fleshtone and fill in the ears.

The Art of Painting Animals on Rocks

Back.

Front.

7 Adding Fur Lines.

You're now ready to begin the delicate fur lines that will give your kitten its fluffy look. Follow the directional guide above to create realistic fur lines.

Starting with the gold section of the haunch, fill in a series of short, fine fur lines with burnt sienna. Use your smallest brush. Work from inside to outside in shingled layers. Don't be afraid to vary the stroke direction, allowing strokes to cross or overlap.

Use the same burnt sienna to stroke long, contrasting fur lines in the ears. Next, turn the stone and stroke in a series of short, fine lines radiating outward from around the eye on the gold side of the face. Also use burnt sienna to make fine fur lines on the gold areas of the tail and down the gold patch on the back.

Rinse your brush and mix gold with white paint to get a pale straw color. Use this to go over the same patches you just touched up with burnt sienna. Use this paler color sparingly, mainly to highlight and soften the edges of the gold patches. Make short, delicate strokes around the eye. Draw out slender tips of color along the edge of the kitten's cheek and across the top of the

head. Go along the curve of the haunch with the same kind of spiky strokes, keeping them perpendicular to the line of the haunch.

Finally, highlight the edges of the tail, and add fuzz to the outlined ear.

Clean your brush and switch to pale gray by mixing a small amount of black into white. Use this gray to highlight the black patches on your kitten. On the black side of the face radiate lines out from around the kitten's eye and along the top of the head. Shingle fur strokes sparingly along the lower half of the black portion of the haunch. Continue to cover all the black areas in this fashion. Use this same pale gray sparingly to soften and add texture to the white areas also (without making your patches look more like gray patches). Leave the tops of the paws totally white but create a shadow by making gray fur strokes along the bottom edges. Use fine, dark gray lines to smooth the transition between white and black bands of fur. Next add more black to get a deeper shade of gray. Use this color to define the muzzle with a series of short, spoke-like strokes. Add a few lines of small dots across each muzzle to resemble follicles for the whiskers.

Brown lines radiate around the eye.

Texture the haunch with spiky strokes.

Highlight black patches with tiny gray fur lines.

How to Paint a Calico Kitten

8 Eye Detail.

Now you're ready to fill in the eye color. Most kittens' eyes range in color from milky blue-gray to yellow-green. For this kitten I used a medium green softened with burnt sienna. Be sure to leave a black rim showing all the way around each eye. While the eyes are still wet, dip your brush into a drop of gold paint and make an inner ring. Clean and dry your brush and use the tip to draw spikes of gold like sunrays out into the green. Allow the eye color to dry before painting in the football-shaped irises. Let the iris hang down from the top of the eye as though the kitten were looking up.

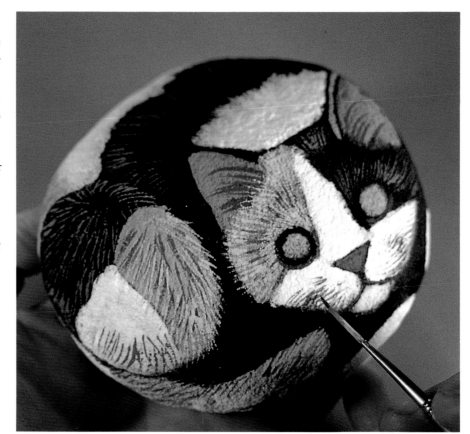

Whisker detail.

Eye detail.

The Art of Painting Animals on Rocks

9 Finishing Touches.

Clean your brush once more and switch to white paint. Fan delicate white ear whiskers out over the darker set you made earlier. Next, soften the blaze between the kitten's eyes by feathering little fur lines along each side. You may find it easier to do these strokes if you turn your kitten around.

To make the whiskers, you may need to dilute the white paint slightly to insure it will flow in long, unbroken lines. Start your whiskers just inside the muzzle area and pull them out in graceful curves. Three or four whiskers per side should be enough.

The final touch is the dot of white at the edge of the iris in each eye.

As with all artwork, you should sign your finished piece and seal the painted surfaces.

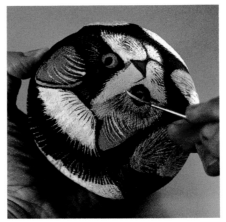

Soften the blaze with tiny lines.

Bring your kitten to life with a white sparkle in each eye.

While single kittens are cute enough, two or three kittens in a basket or posed on a pillow are even more enchanting. Once you have mastered this first design, try making up variations by changing the patches. You may also use the same basic steps to create all-white or all-black kittens. If you enjoyed this project, start collecting pictures of kittens and try your hand at different breeds. Kitten calendars, cat food ads or magazines like *Cat Fancy* are all good sources for pictures to begin your own library of images.

A variety of breeds.

The Art of Painting Animals on Rocks

How to Paint a
Gray Persian

Persian cats are known for their elegance and regal bearing. This smokey gray Persian looks best on a fairly large stone (at least 10″ to 12″ in overall length).

The crouching position requires an upright stone. It is particularly important that the stone have a smooth, vertical front side. When searching for a suitable stone, think in terms of a narrow loaf shape, that is, one that's rather squared off at either end. Or you might look for an oval stone with a flat bottom. If the stone tilts slightly, use the side that slopes backward as the front for best visibility.

A suitable Persian cat rock.

What You'll Need

- black, white, red, yellow and blue acrylic paints
- large, medium and narrow bristle brushes
- a pencil
- measuring tape (optional)

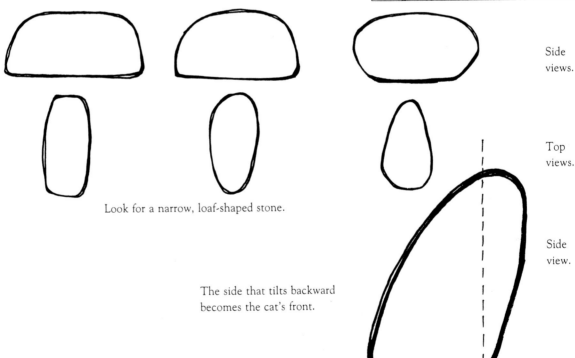

Side views.

Top views.

Side view.

Look for a narrow, loaf-shaped stone.

The side that tilts backward becomes the cat's front.

1 The Base Coat.

Prepare your rock's surface for painting with a thorough scrubbing. To make a medium gray, gradually add small amounts of white paint to a tablespoon-sized puddle of black until you reach a middle value. Use this color and your largest brush to completely cover the exposed surface of the stone. Allow this base coat to dry before beginning your layout.

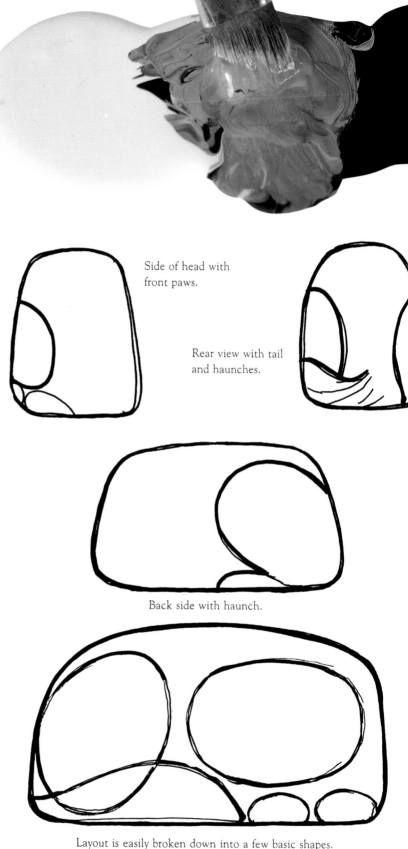

2 Basic Shapes.

Sketch an oval head at one end of your stone midway between top and bottom. This oval should be approximately half as long as the overall length of the stone. The haunch is also an oval about the same size as the head, but set at a 90-degree angle tilting away from the head. Leave at least ½" between the face oval and the edge of the haunch. Begin the tail at the far side of the stone just below the haunch. The tail should sweep like a plume from around the end of the stone, slightly overlapping the haunch before tapering off in a line parallel to the curve of the face. Don't allow the tail's tip to extend into the area below the cat's chin. You will need that space for the paws. Form the paws by sketching two half circles side by side directly below the head. Extend the outer paw sideways around the end of the stone so it tapers off into the bottom edge of the stone.

Side of head with front paws.

Rear view with tail and haunches.

Back side with haunch.

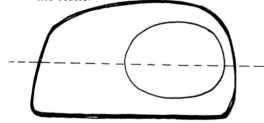

Center the head on an imaginary horizontal midline.

Layout is easily broken down into a few basic shapes.

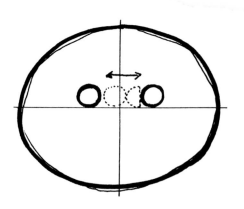 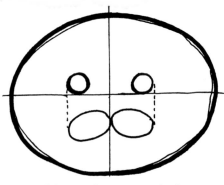 

Facial features begin as simple shapes.

3 Face Layout.

To insure proper placement of the cat's features, divide the face in quarters. Persian cats' eyes are round (⅝" in diameter on my 11" cat). Their bottom edges should rest on the horizontal center line. Leave a distance of one and a half eye widths between the two eyes, and be sure they are equidistant from the sides of the face.

Move straight down from the outside edge of each eye. This line defines the outer edge of the muzzle area. Set two oval shapes angled toward each other, meeting at the vertical midline.

To render the ears, start at the midpoint of each eye and move up in a straight line. That point on either side marks where the inside edge of the ear should go. As a rule, Persians have the shortest ears in the cat family while Siamese cats have the largest. Sketch in the ears as triangles.

Another characteristic of the Persian breed is its short nose. Tuck a small triangle into the space where the two muzzle ovals come together. From the bottom of this triangle extend another short line down, then allow it to split to form the mouth.

Outlining the features.

Establish your cat's contours.

4 Painting the Contours.

With your medium brush and black paint, outline the shapes of the head, haunch, tail and paws. Remember to turn your stone around and outline the back haunch and the extension of the outer paw as well. Use your smallest brush to outline the eyes, nose and mouth lines. The eyes will look more lifelike if you extend lines down from the inside corners.

Switch to your bigger brush and blacken the contours between the head and haunch. Feather your strokes out from the top of the head. Do a second band of feathered strokes farther back to indicate the cat's shoulder blades. Curve this band in so it nearly touches the first band directly behind the head. Fill in all the spaces between the paws and the head with black. Paint several long, flowing lines along the length of the tail. With your medium-sized brush radiate shorter black lines like uneven spokes around the lower portion of the haunch.

Do a set of similar strokes fanning outward around the eyes and smudge the lines with your fingers. Leave an area of plain gray base coat showing directly below the eyes, but emphasize the shape of the muzzle with dark smudges as shown. Add texture to the cat's back with similar, heavy brushstrokes.

Build contrast with bold brushstrokes.

Contour the back with heavy marks.

Steps to build eye color.

5 Facial Feature Details.

Using your medium brush, mix white and red to get a medium pink. Fill in the nose triangle. Now add a touch of black and more white to tone down the pink. Use this softer shade to fill in the insides of the ears.

Clean your brush well before mixing eye colors. I used yellow with a touch of white to get a soft, creamy hue. While the eyes are still wet, add a touch of blue to your paint puddle to get a blue-green. Use this to paint an upside-down *U* shape of color inside each eye. Then mix a touch of black into the blue-green and radiate thin lines of this deeper shade out from the center of each eye. Allow the eye color to dry before centering the irises in black. While you have black on your brush, fan a set of dark fur lines out from the inside corners of both ears.

Fleshing in the ears.

Eye detail.

Ear detail.

The Art of Painting Animals on Rocks

Directions for fur patches (rear).

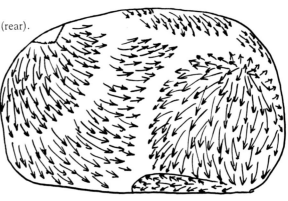

Direction for fur patches (front).

Crisscross.

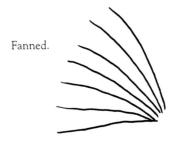

Fanned.

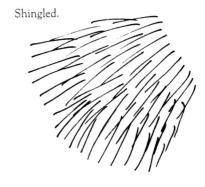

Shingled.

6 Adding Texture.

To begin stroking on your fur lines, mix white paint to the proper consistency for fine lines and use a script liner with a clean, sharp point. You will use several different types of strokes. Follow the directional guide shown. Begin along the inside curve of the haunch and stroke lines outward in assorted lengths, varying the direction so that some overlap. Then work into the interior of the haunch and begin shingling another set of longer tapering lines so the ends blend into the first set. Keep shingling in rows, remembering to cross and overlap in a random fashion. If your strokes are too uniform, your cat will appear more stylized than realistic. Turn your stone around and render the back haunch in a similar fashion.

The fur lines along the tail are even longer and more flowing. Begin at the base of the tail and make strokes that fan outward along its length. There should be a minimum of crossing strokes here as you want the tail fur to appear sleek and silky.

To detail the face, use dense, short strokes and follow the curves like spokes on a wheel. Shingle a second layer over the first.

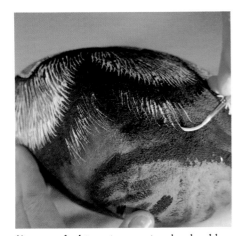

You may find it easier to paint the shoulders from the back.

Fur lines on the tail are long and flowing.

Leave a ring of gray base color around each eye.

How to Paint a Gray Persian

Render the muzzle with short, prickly strokes.

Tiny herringbone pattern lines accent the ears.

Clarify the cat's chin with fan-shaped strokes. Move on to the muzzle and paint in a similar fashion. All strokes should radiate away from the nose.

Now encircle the eyes. Begin at the upper inside corner and work out and around, leaving a fringe of the gray base paint showing around the outer edge of each eye.

To work on the bridge of your cat's nose, you may find it helpful to turn the stone upside down. Stroke an hourglass-shaped set of lines from the nose upward between the eyes. Try to leave darker lines on either side of the nose to define its shape. Next, using very delicate lines, highlight the angles of the ears. You can get a nice effect with a herringbone pattern of tiny strokes along the edge.

7 Detailing the Back.

Complete the fur strokes on your cat by highlighting the shoulder blade areas. Begin just past the neck, leaving a dark border area for contrast between back and head. Fan your strokes out, working away from the head. You may find it more natural to stroke these lines on if you turn your stone around and work from the back. Leave a ragged curving area of black for contrast. Do a second set of shingled strokes behind the inside shoulder blade area following the contours of your stone to the base of the tail. From the outside shoulder blade, let your rows of fur strokes flow in a fanning pattern down the back. Again, remember to leave a contrasting border of black between these areas and the haunch. To detail the paws, tilt your stone or prop it at an angle. Outline all the paws with short, spiky lines.

Look your cat over from every angle for sufficient detail. If there doesn't seem to be enough contrast between the head or the haunch and the rest of the cat, use a bit of watery black paint to tint the surrounding fur so the lighter areas stand out.

Remember to leave a black outline around the haunch for contrast.

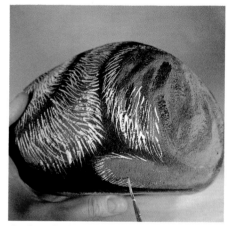
Outline the back paw with short, spiky lines.

The Art of Painting Animals on Rocks

8 Finishing Touches.

While you have black on your brush, touch up any place where fur lines may need more definition. Dot several rows of whisker follicles across each muzzle.

Clean your brush thoroughly and dilute white paint so it flows on easily yet has enough pigment to remain opaque as it dries. Use this paint to stroke on three or four whiskers from each side of the muzzle. You may have to go over your whiskers more than once to make them stand out. Apply similar long lines along the insides of the ears. Finally, with a dot of thick white paint, place a sparkle in the iris of each eye.

As with all your work, sign it at the bottom and seal the painted surfaces. These Persian cats can be displayed just about anywhere. If your stone isn't too wide, try setting it on a window sill, perch it on a stair or anywhere else a real cat might choose to survey his kingdom. Using the same basic techniques, you can try your hand at other long-haired cats — a creamy Himalayan with brown face markings or a solid white Persian with details in shades of gray.

Whisker detail.

Clarify your fur patches with fine black lines.

Add dots to suggest whisker follicles.

A pair of pampered Persians.

The Art of Painting Animals on Rocks

How to Paint a
Yellow-Striped
Tabby Cat

This project is similar to the calico kitten, but requires a larger stone. The proportions will differ also as adult, short-haired cats generally have smaller heads in comparison to body size. The stone I chose for this project measures 11″ across. It's 4″ high and fairly round in shape. Other suitable stones might be thicker or more dome-shaped on top. They could also be oval or kidney-shaped instead of round.

Prepare your stone for painting by making sure it is clean and dry.

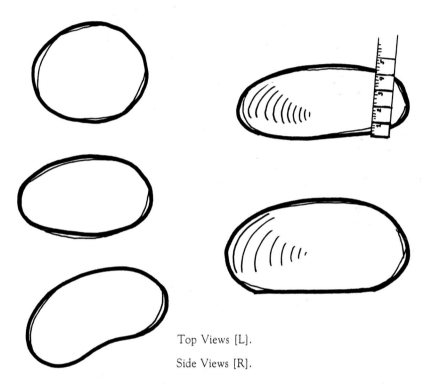

Top Views [L].

Side Views [R].

A tabby stone will be larger than a calico kitten stone.

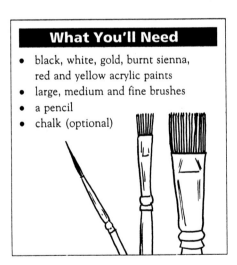

What You'll Need

- black, white, gold, burnt sienna, red and yellow acrylic paints
- large, medium and fine brushes
- a pencil
- chalk (optional)

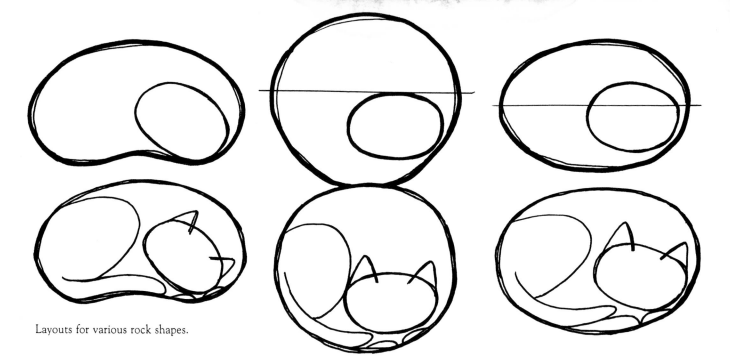

Layouts for various rock shapes.

1 Layout.

Turn your stone slowly around and decide on the best site for the head. Even a uniformly rounded stone usually presents one side with a slightly smoother surface or a more even plane. The head can be placed to the right or the left side of the stone.

On my 11"-wide stone the head oval is not quite 4½" across by 3¾" high. If you use an oval stone you may want to make the head slightly larger, or simply leave more space between the cat's head and haunch to make up the difference.

The position of the head will vary with the shape of the stone. Just be sure to leave enough room for the outside ear on the side of the head. For kidney-shaped stones, the crook represents the curve between head and haunch.

On my cat, the base of the ear triangles measure 1½", while the sides are 2" long. Ear size differs from breed to breed, and from cat to cat, so exact measurements are less important than how the ears look on your cat. As a rule, leave a space between the ears equal to at least the width of one ear.

Make the cat's haunch oval an inch or so larger than the head, and set it at an angle to the head. The tail begins below and behind the haunch and wraps around the lower edge of the stone, curving up slightly so the tip is aimed at the cat's chin. The paws are two elongated ovals that meet below and to one side of the head oval.

To set guidelines for the face, divide the head into quarters. The bottoms of the eyes should rest on top of the horizontal line. Like the ears, a cat's eye size can vary. If the eyes are too large,

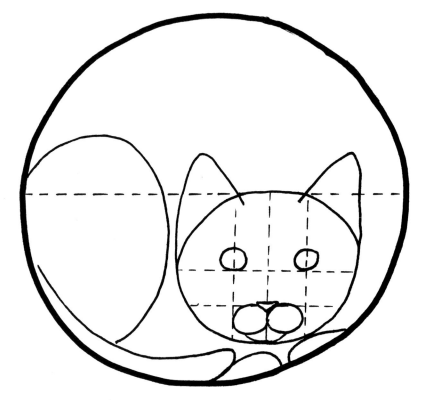

Face layout.

The Art of Painting Animals on Rocks

however, you risk making your cat look more like a cartoon kitty than a real one. On my stone the eyes are round and measure a little less than an inch across. They are spaced a full inch apart on the face. Generally speaking, it's better to have the eyes set a bit too wide than too close.

Draw another horizontal line between the chin and the horizontal midline. The top line of the nose triangle should be even with this second line. Draw two circles for the muzzle and a half-moon to create the chin.

Ready to paint.

2 Contours.

Use your medium-sized brush and black paint to outline the head and ears, haunch, tail and paws. You may use the same brush or your smaller one to outline the facial features. Darken the space between the paws and the chin. Next use your biggest brush to quickly fill in the contours between the head and haunch. Feather this contour shadowing up as far as the tip on the inside ear. This may seem like too much black right now, but later you will blend your cat's stripes into the area and soften that effect.

Painting in the shadows.

3 Base Coat.

Rinse out your large brush, then cover the unpainted surfaces of your stone with burnt sienna, leaving only the eyes, muzzle and, if you like, some stripes on the tail unpainted. Be careful not to paint over your black outlines on the face. If you do so accidently, be sure to retouch them later.

Turn your stone as you paint, making certain you cover every surface that shows. Allow this base coat to dry.

Painting on the base coat.

How to Paint a Yellow-Striped Tabby Cat

4 Basic Stripes.

For the stripes use a medium-sized flat brush. I prefer an older brush whose bristles have separated with age. This allows me to create a distinct fur texture with each stroke. If you don't have a brush like this, apply stripes in solid but ragged lines. You can go back over them later and add texture with a contrasting color.

Mix gold paint with a bit of white to get a pale, sandy color. You cat's stripes may be uniform or more uneven and broken. If you aren't sure how to do the stripes, try sketching them in with chalk first and curving them to create the illusion of roundness to the haunch. Next, turn your stone around and begin the back stripes in two sets an inch or so beyond the top of the head. Leave a strip of the darker base coat at the nape of the neck and running down along the curve of the spine until it disappears around the edge of stone. The back stripes should be an inch or so wide, curving gently around the shoulders.

Use the same pale gold and your medium or smallest brush to paint in the pattern of facial stripes as shown. Fill in the muzzle are as well.

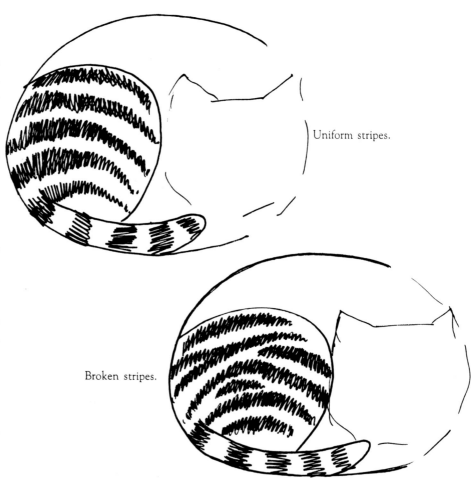

Uniform stripes.

Broken stripes.

Without rinsing out your brush, switch to plain white paint and stroke in the lighter stripes along the cat's tail and the tips of the cat's paws. Make several narrower stripes along the front legs also. Encircle the eyes with white, and make two small white patches on the muzzle just below the nose. Also paint in the chin area with white.

Painting the haunch stripes.

Leave a strip of base coat showing between the stripes on your cat's back.

The Art of Painting Animals on Rocks

Next mix your white paint with a hint of red to get a pale pink. Add a touch of gold to soften the shade to a pinkish fleshtone and fill in the insides of the ears. Add more red to deepen the hue and fill in the nose. With your thinnest brush, carefully line the lower curve of each eye between the black inner circle and the white outer circle.

Facial stripe patterns.

Softening the features.

5 Softening With Details.

It's time to paint the delicate details that give your stone cat its touchably soft appearance. Begin by mixing burnt sienna with just enough black to get a deep chocolate brown.

The Face

Make a row of dark fur lines starting at the base of the ears and fanning out as they move up along the inside edges. With very short, fine lines, indicate all the darker areas of your cat's face. Bring out the bridge of the cat's nose by painting a dark line on either side running from the tip of the nose to the inside corners of the eyes. Also be sure to outline the eyes and the tip of the nose. Add definition to the curve of the muzzle by encircling both sides with small, spoke-like strokes. Next make three sets of horizontal, dotted lines across the muzzle on each side. These indicate the follicles for the whiskers.

The Body

Using your small brush and the adjacent guide for fur stroke direction, add dark fur strokes to the body of the cat. Turn your stone around so the back side is facing you and begin at the top of the head between the ears. Feather your strokes and allow them to blend

Face detail.

Follow the arrows for fur patterns.

Blend the stripes with fine strokes in dark brown and gold for a natural finish.

Stubbly white lines create contrast around the head.

slightly into the lighter gold stripes. Don't make your lines too uniform. Vary their length and direction for a more natural look. Continue striping back in this way until you reach the bottom edge of the stone.

Turn your stone to the front and, with the same dark brown, define the stripes on the haunch. Every dark stripe should be hatched with a series of close, fine lines extending both above and below the stripe to create a

soft, blended effect. Intersperse a few brown lines in the gold stripes to break up their solid look. Do the same thing on the tail.

When you have done enough of these darker fur lines, clean your brush. Pour a small amount of white and a small amount of gold paint onto your palette. Keep the two colors separate. Alternate between the two, blending in fur lines the same way you just did with the dark lines. When you have

added enough highlights to the body stripes, do a series of short, splinterlike strokes that bristle out following the contours of the haunch. Now you are ready to move on to the face.

Outline the angles of the ears with white or very pale gold so they stand out clearly. Then, with the same pale gold/white encircle the entire head with tight splinterlike strokes.

Paint the eyes in three steps.

6 The Eyes.

Mix a small amount of yellow paint with white to create a buttery shade. Use this color to fill in the eye circles. Be careful not to cover up the black outlines around the eyes. (If you do stray over them, wait until the paint is dry to redefine them with black.)

While the yellow paint is still wet, fill the tip of your brush with burnt sienna and shadow the upper portion of the eye with a series of thin strokes. The shadow should take the shape of an inverted *U*.

After the eyes have dried, use a

clean brush and black paint to place the oval-shaped irises in the center of each eye. I like to allow the iris to touch the top of the eye circle so the cat appears to be looking up. Add sparkle to each iris with a dot of thick white paint.

7 Finishing Touches.

To complete your cat, add just enough water to your white paint to get a consistency that will flow on smoothly yet remain opaque. Extend four or five long, curving whiskers outward from each side of the muzzle area. The lower whiskers may overlap the tail or the paws. Make another set of long, graceful lines inside the ears.

At this point examine your cat from every angle to see if touching up is needed. Pay particular attention to easily overlooked areas like the side of the stone just beyond the outside edge of the head. Determine if the paws require some additional texture. You may use the tip of your brush to stroke a line of white fuzz along the tops of them. The whiskers may need going over more than once to insure that they stand out clearly. Or you can bring them out nicely by painting a narrow line of black along the bottom of each one.

You can adapt these techniques to any number of curled-up cat rocks. Try a sleeping cat with its eyes closed in contented crescents; or change the base coat to deep brown, make the lighter stripes tan and the fur lines black to paint a brown tiger cat. These cats look especially nice displayed in baskets or curled onto pillows. Experiment with stripe patterns and collect photos of cats to help you achieve a more realistic look.

Whisker detail.

A cat on a lap.

The Art of Painting Animals on Rocks

How to Paint a
Raccoon

W hether real or stone, these little masked bandits are apt to steal away the hardest of hearts. With their mischievous antics and comical faces, live raccoons have won widespread popularity. They also make terrific subjects for rock painting because so many different stone shapes work for them.

The most common shape, and the one demonstrated here, is an upright, half-circle-shaped stone. It can be uniformly curved on top, slightly squared off, or perhaps even sloping to one side. Occasionally I run across what I call a "tombstone"-type rock, one which is bluntly rounded but stands taller. These rocks are ideal for painting a "raccoon" as though it has reared up on its hind legs, with the front paws held to its chest. It's OK for a raccoon rock to be on the narrow side, but any stones less than 4″ thick will be too thin. Since you have many choices, try to envision some ways an animal can be fitted to various shapes and sizes.

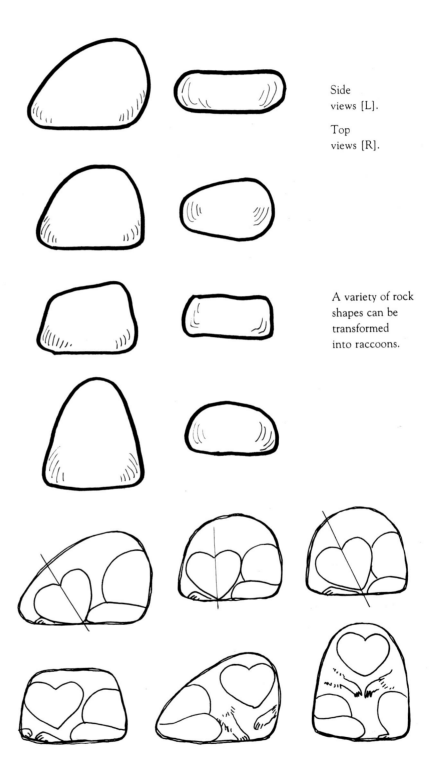

Side views [L].

Top views [R].

A variety of rock shapes can be transformed into raccoons.

Your layout will depend on the dimensions of your stone.

Prepare your stone for painting by insuring the surface is clean and free of loose material or debris.

Before you begin your layout, use your largest brush and black paint to completely cover the surface of the stone, leaving only the bottom unpainted. Let this base coat dry thoroughly.

Selecting your rock.

The base coat.

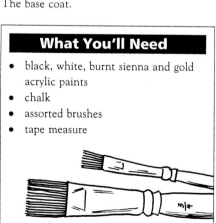

1 Layout.

The proportions for a crouching pose will differ from those for a standing animal. Generally, the head takes up a larger percentage of the stone in a crouched pose (roughly half the width of the stone). In an upright pose the raccoon's head will take up less space in proportion to overall body size (usually a little over ⅓).

Positioning the head is the first and most important step of the layout process. The head can be set level or tilted slightly, as I have done. On sloping stones where there is not much room, tilting the head may be the best solution for fitting the ears into the available space. Another option is to place the head on the higher side and fit the haunch onto the sloping end.

The head will be shaped like a short, fat heart. On my 9″ stone, this heart measures 4″ across the top. Use chalk to sketch in your head until it looks right. The haunch is similar in size to the head, but circular instead of heart shaped. Let it curve around the end of the stone. The tail is fat with a blunt tip. Bring it around from the end of the stone, stopping just short of the head. If you have postioned your head high enough, sketch in a front paw under the chin.

Note that raccoons' front feet (on page 63) look almost like small human hands while the rear feet are longer with shorter toes. Turn your stone around and make a matching haunch on the back side with a little bit of the long back foot showing. Now you are ready to begin sketching in facial details.

Begin with several basic shapes.

The Art of Painting Animals on Rocks

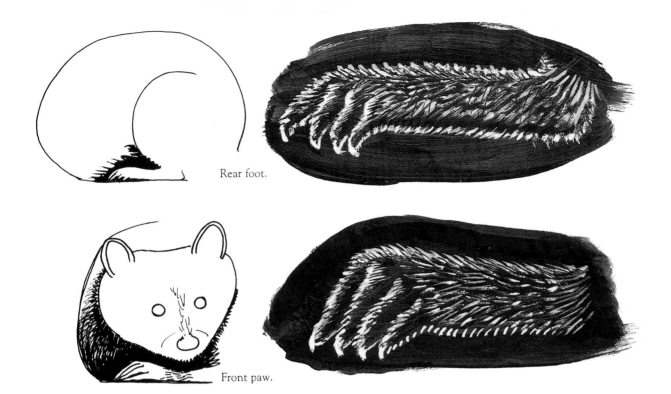

Rear foot.

Front paw.

Face Layout

Divide the heart-shaped face in thirds vertically. If you opted to tilt the head, angle the lines to match. Set the ears so their inside corners touch the lines you've drawn. Raccoon ears vary in size depending on the age of the animal. Here, the ears extend a little over 1″ from the top of the head. The total height of one ear should be about equal to the distance between the two ears.

Next, bisect the head horizontally. The raccoon's eyes will be centered on the points where this horizontal line crosses the two vertical lines. Space the eyes slightly less than two eye widths apart. Add triangles to the inside edge of each eye to suggest tear ducts.

Draw another horizontal guideline halfway between the midline and the bottom of the face. This point represents the top edge of the animal's muzzle. The outside perimeters of the muzzle circle are defined by the two vertical lines you made earlier. Draw a circle to create the muzzle.

In the center of the muzzle sketch an oval nose shape. The raccoon's nose should be slightly larger than one of his eyes.

That completes the layout process. Now you are ready to paint.

Ready to paint.

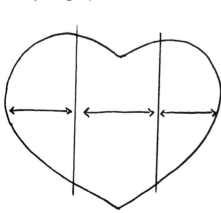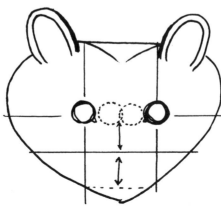

Basic shapes develop the facial features.

2 Fur Patches.

Use your medium brush and white paint to fill in the muzzle area surrounding the nose, but leave a wedge-shaped portion of the black base coat uncovered at the top. Heavily outline the ears with white. Next, without rinsing your brush, add several drops of gold paint to your dish and soften it to a pale straw color with white. Use this color to brush in three or four vertical bands along the raccoon's tail. These bands should be ½" to ¾" wide with ragged edges.

Tail bands.

The fur lines are next. Study the directional guide above to determine the general pattern.

Using your narrowest brush and plain white paint, begin your first lines at the inside corner of each eye. Your strokes should be nearly solid at the base, but should fan out above the eye. Lengthen and angle your strokes as you move around toward the side of the face. Blend a second tier of fur lines into the first, allowing your tapering strokes to vary slightly in length and direction as they fill in the remaining area below the ear.

Move to the other eye and repeat these steps. Leave a blank space in the middle of the forehead as an extension of the dark area above the nose and between the eyes. Also leave a narrow

Front.

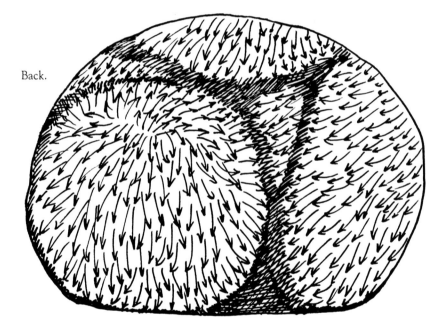

Back.

Painting the tail step-by-step.

The Art of Painting Animals on Rocks

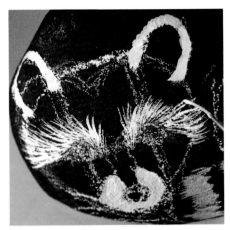

Feathery brushstrokes surround the eyes.

Outline the entire face with short, prickly strokes.

Filling in the haunch.

border of black showing at the base of the ears to insure they stand out.

Next, define and detail the shape of the head. Begin at the top of the head between the ears and stroke a line of short, spiky fur straight across.

Continue the process all the way around the chin and up the other side.

Use the same type of "prickly" stroke to outline the outside perimeters of the haunch. Then work from bottom to top filling in the remaining

area of the haunch with shingle-type strokes of varying lengths and angles. The more delicate and numerous your fur lines, the more realistic your finished piece will be, so take your time and do a thorough job.

3 Using the Base Coat for Contrast.

To enhance the illusion of volume, indicate the curve of your raccoon's shoulders above the head. Do this by leaving a ½"-band of the dark base coat showing behind the head. Fan several rows of white fur lines out in the half-round areas surrounding each ear. Be careful to leave a strip of the dark base-coat showing around the ears also for contrast. Allow your brush strokes to cross or overlap here and there.

Continue back with a second set of fur lines, following the curving shape of the rock around until you reach the back haunch on one side and the bottom of the stone on the other. From the back, this second set should resemble a double U. There will be a triangular space between the two U-shaped areas above the back haunch. You may fill it in sparingly, but leave a border of basecoat showing around it.

Leave a strip of base coat surrounding the ears.

How to Paint a Raccoon

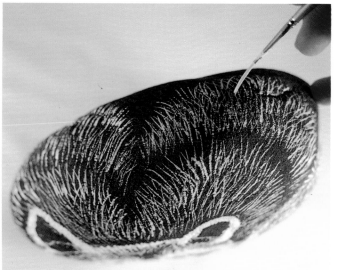

Fur on the shoulder blades takes the shape of an M.

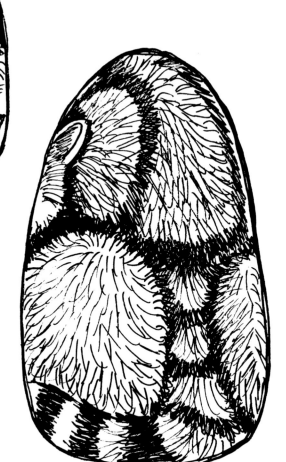

Rear haunch fur pattern.

Fill in the back haunch shape just like the front one, again leaving a contrasting strip of black all around. Now turn your stone sideways and fill in the narrow space between the haunches. Use several sets of fan-shaped fur clusters, leaving dark borders around each set. At the other end of your stone, stroke fur lines out and away from the face until they blend into the strokes coming down from the shoulder.

Examine your piece from every angle. Add crisscrossing strokes where needed to break up any fur lines that seem too uniform. Make sure you left borders for contrast around all your contours. You may heighten this contrast by adding more fine, white fur lines around the face and haunch. Use "prickly"-type strokes to soften the ears and the outside of the muzzle.

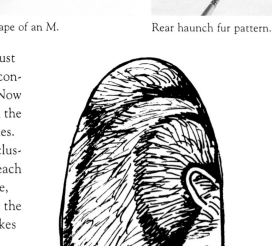

Head end.

Soften the ears and muzzle with delicate lines.

Tail end.

The Art of Painting Animals on Rocks

4 The Eyes.

The eyes should now be the last unpainted portion of your stone raccoon. Real raccoons' eyes are so dark they seem black, but I paint them dark brown so they stand out from the surrounding black mask. Mix a brushful of burnt sienna with a tinge of black to get a deep chocolate brown. Carefully fill in the eye circles with this color. While they are still wet, dip the tip of your brush into a drop of straight burnt sienna and stroke it sparingly in a half-circle around the lower half of the eyes. This warms the eyes, giving them depth and clarity. While they dry, go around the outside of the eyes with a delicate line of black to emphasize their shape. Add a very thin eyelid line just above either eye as well. While you have black on your brush, look for areas where your fur lines may need separating or redefining. A few thin black strokes can correct white fur lines that look blotchy or are too thick.

Filling in the eyes.

5 Detailing the Face.

Clean your brush and return to straight burnt sienna. Use this color to make a fringe along the top of each eye. Stroke in a few longer lines along the inside corners of the eyes and both ears. Do a similar fringe around the top half of the muzzle and sprinkle more reddish-brown strokes up into the bridge of the nose.

Add texture to the light stripes on the tail with a series of brown horizontal strokes. Turn your raccoon on his side and sprinkle some brown fur along his front and rear paws.

Now add enough gold paint to your burnt sienna to get a warm golden-brown. Use this color to soften the black mask below each eye with fine lines.

Clean your brush, switch to black paint and carefully place an oval iris into the center of each eye so it just touches the top of the eye circle.

At first, the face is only black and white.

Add highlights with burnt sienna.

Blending the tail fur for a sleek look.

Speckle touches of golden-brown under the eyes and on the bridge of the nose.

Face detail with color highlights.

Tinting the shoulders.

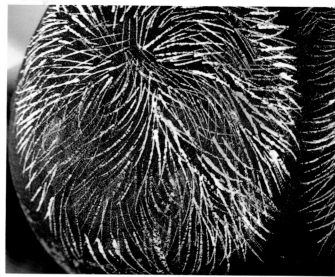
Tinting the haunch.

6 Tinting the Fur.

Right now your animal's fur is primarily black and white. By diluting a combination of burnt sienna and gold, you can make a translucent wash to tint your white fur lines in selected areas. Saturate your large brush so it is full, but not dripping. Place a small amount of gold paint next to an equal portion of burnt sienna and use your wet brush to mix the two. Add several drops of water to the paint and do a test swatch on newspaper. If the paint is the right consistency, it will tint the paper without covering the printing.

Brush the tint across the shoulder behind the head. The white fur lines should change to a pale golden-red color. If the paint is not diluted enough, the black areas will be tinted as well. If this happens, simply dab up the excess pigment with a tissue and try adding more water to your paint.

The best areas to tint are those just beyond the head and ears and around the haunches. Tinting creates a more natural look. Avoid tinting any white fur lines that you depend on for high contrast.

Brown and gold face highlights.

7 Finishing Touches.

Use white paint and your smallest brush to outline the front and rear paws with dense, fine fur. Highlight all fingers and toes with this fuzz, and sprinkle more white fur lines down the length of the paws.

To finish the nose, paint two white slits for nostrils. Then soften your white paint to gray and add a pale gleam across the top. Darken this gray and use it to encircle the muzzle with distinct fur lines so it stands out clearly from the rest of the face.

For the whiskers, mix just enough water into white paint to get a consistency that can be drawn out without skipping. Paint five long, curving whiskers on each side of the muzzle. Fill the insides of both ears with whiskers as well, fanning them out from the

Nose detail.

Whisker detail.

The Art of Painting Animals on Rocks

A completed raccoon (rear view).

Front view

Side view.

inside corners. Finally, dab a dot of white paint to form a sparkle in each eye.

Your completed raccoon is now ready to be signed and sealed.

People frequently ask if they can display their painted stones outside. The answer is a qualified yes! I have had a life-sized raccoon next to my front door welcoming visitors for several years with no sign of deterioration. However, I recommend that stone art have some protection from the elements. Mine is under a covered porch away from direct sunlight and dampness. Stones placed directly on the ground may soak up moisture, causing the paint to flake or fade.

Raccoon rocks can be practically any size. I paint a lot of "kit raccoons" on kitten-sized stones. Baby raccoons are similar to mature ones, but with rounder heads, shorter muzzles and skinnier tails. The eyes are also larger in proportion to their heads. As with other projects in this book, I suggest you try to collect reference photos to help you achieve realism in your work.

A family of raccoons—waiting for a picnic.

The Art of Painting Animals on Rocks

How to Paint a
Stone Fawn

At first glance it's easy to mistake this stone fawn for the real thing. Sitting so still, its long legs tucked neatly underneath, it tempts you to watch and see if it blinks. Fawns fold themselves into exquisitely compact positions. You could hardly ask for a better subject to paint on stone.

I'm particular about the stones I use for fawns. The ideal shape is a plump oval angled at one end to simulate the crook of the fawn's back leg. Unfortunately these stones aren't always easy to find. For this demonstration, I have chosen a plain, elongated oval-shaped stone that is much more common.

the shores of the Great Lakes. The fawn turned out fine, but lifting it required two people. I wouldn't recommend working that large. Most of my fawns measure between 9″ and 24″ in length. The one in this demonstration is 13″ across.

When you have selected your rock, scrub it down and let it dry.

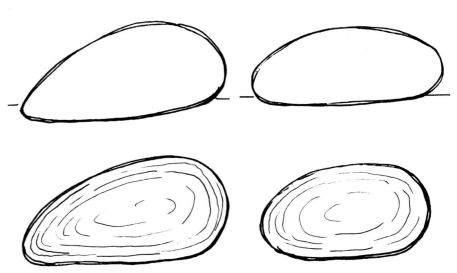

The best fawn rocks are oval or egg-shaped.

Fawn stones may be done fairly flat or in a more rounded version. However, flat stones look best when viewed from above, while rounder stones look good from several angles. Like so many stone animals, they can be painted in a wide range of sizes, from a pebble that fits in an outstretched palm to near boulder size. I once painted a fawn on a huge granite rock brought to me from

A good-sized fawn stone.

1 Basic Layout.

The length of your fawn's head (from between the ears to the tip of the nose) should be approximately half of the stone's overall length. The length of the ears often dictates the placement of the head. A good rule of thumb is to make the ears three-fourths as long as the head. That means that on my 13″ rock, the head measures 6½″ so the ears should be a shade over 4½″. (1) Remember that none of these measurements is "carved in stone." They are included only to help you proportion the animal's features to one another.

Start by bisecting your stone lengthwise. On the side you've designated for the head, follow this line to where it's just about to curve around the edge of the stone. That point marks the tip of the outer ear. (2) Move your pencil back down the line the length of one ear and mark that spot. This point is where the base of the ear joins the top of the head. From there measure off the length of the head at a 45-degree angle from the midline. If you aren't sure how to determine a 45-degree angle, lightly sketch in a square, using the point on the midline where the ear begins as the upper corner. Cut across the square diagonally from that point to the opposite corner to establish a 45-degree angle. (3) Next, from the nose end of the head line you just made, move your pencil back up an inch or so and cross it with a short perpendicular line. This line should be about one-fourth as long as the length of the head. On my stone that makes it a little over 1½″. Now go back to the point that marks the top of the head. Make a second perpendicular line (like the top of a capital T). (4) Connect the points of the T with the nose end. You should end up with a four-sided shape that resembles a wedge. (5) Lop

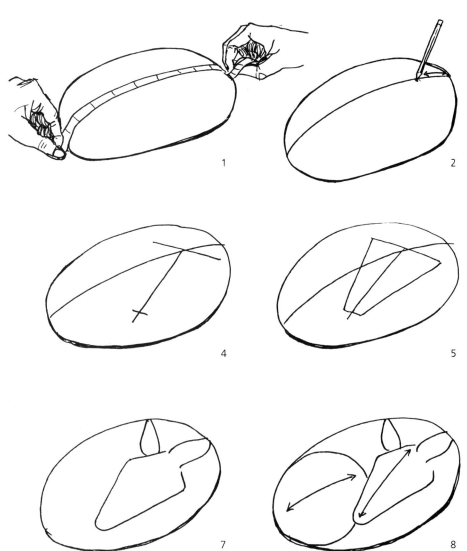

off the two top corners at 45-degree angles to round the top of the head. At the nose end, draw a half-circle to form a muzzle. (6) The inside ear is centered in the upper angle at the top of the head. Both ears should be about the same length, but the inside one has a curving front side and a straight back edge. (7) (see next page) Before refining the head shape further, sketch in an oval haunch. Its length along the stone's midline is equal to the length of the head. Depending on the shape of your stone, the fawn's nose may touch or even overlap the haunch.

(8) The hind leg forms an *L* shape along the bottom edge of the stone. If your stone has a distinct curve along this edge, you will have to keep the hind leg from looking like it bows out. Sketch the leg in at an upward-tilting angle cutting straight across the rock. (9) You can minimize this curve later by blacking out the area directly below the leg. The end of the leg has another small downward crook for an ankle, and the hoof is similar to a small rectangle that has been split. The tips of the hooves should tilt slightly upward.

The space between the jawline and

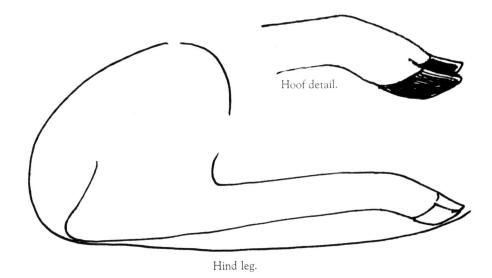

Hoof detail.

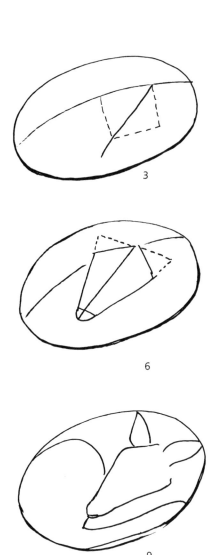

3

6

9

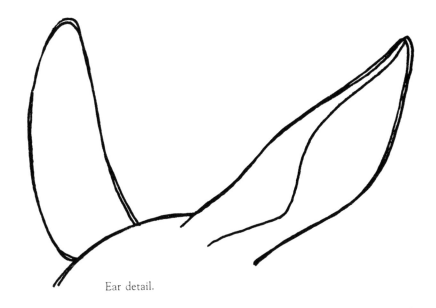

Hind leg.

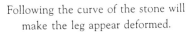

Following the curve of the stone will make the leg appear deformed.

Hind leg should cut across the stone in a straight line.

hind leg will vary depending on the thickness of your stone. If there is room, you may want to add a folded front leg above the hind leg.

To indicate the curve of the fawn's body, sweep a line back from behind the inner ear to form the neck. Run a second line from the upper edge of the outside ear parallel to the first line. The throat line is an extension of the jawline, curving back into the base.

Turn your stone to the tail end and sketch in an oval tail with a pointed tip.

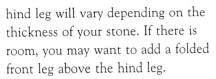

Ear detail.

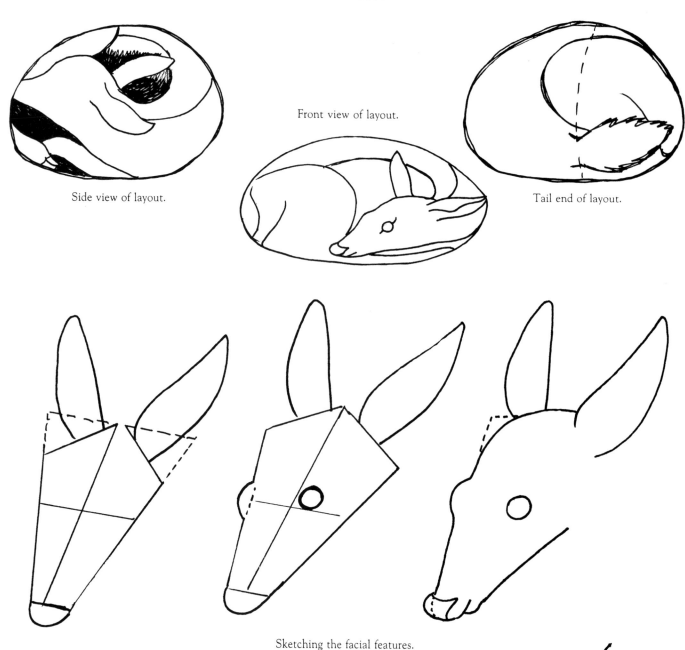

Side view of layout.

Front view of layout.

Tail end of layout.

Sketching the facial features.

The Face

Since the head is at a three-quarters angle, only one eye will actually show, but the other eye forms a visible bulge. The eyes should fall halfway between the ears and nose. Draw a perpendicular guideline for reference.

A fawn's eyes are large and expressive. Using the line you just made as your guide, tuck an eye circle into the upper right quadrant of your intersecting lines. On my fawn the eye is between ¾" and 1" across. Shape the eye by extending the inside lower corner downward and slanting the opposite outside corner upward. Indicate the other eye by sketching in a corresponding bulge along the left side of the head. Just below the eye, narrow the width of the muzzle so the nose tapers slightly. Draw in the nose and mouth as shown. Now you're ready to paint.

Nose detail.

The Art of Painting Animals on Rocks

2 Painting the Shadows.

With a large or medium brush and black paint, fill in the shadows between the haunch and the inside ear, and behind the ear inside the curving line of the spine. Feather out the shadows as you move away from these features. Outline the ears, the upper haunch, and the space between the chin and hind leg. Also black out any portion showing below the crooked hind leg. This is especially important if your stone has a convex front side that you want to play down. Use your small or medium brush to outline the head and the eye, and to fill the nose and hoof. Paint the tail in black, feathering out your strokes along the edges.

3 Base Color.

Pour two good-sized puddles of burnt sienna and gold into your paint dish. Use your large- or medium-sized brush to mix the two colors in the center, leaving some unmixed pigment on either side. Fill in the haunch and the entire hind leg. Also fill in the head, being careful not to paint over any black outlines. Dip the tip of your brush into the gold side of your paint and stroke highlights along the top edge of the forehead and the top of the outside ear. A little straight gold along the upper curve of the haunch will bring out its shape as well. Clean your brush and dip it into straight burnt sienna. Stroke this color in a curve beginning at the nape of the neck and moving back along the spine all the way around to the base of the tail. Feather a few horizontal strokes here and there in the black area between the haunch and the inside ear to soften the shadows. Use burnt sienna all along the lower edge of the hind leg to give it more volume. Leave the chest area unpainted for now.

Ready to paint.

Painting the shadows.

Burnt sienna serves as a base color.

4 Adding Details.

Color the inner portion of the outside ear next. With a small or medium brush mix white and red paint to get a medium pink, then add just enough gold to soften it to a salmon

Outline the eyes with blended white lines.

Filling the insides of the ears.

Painting the ears.

Outline the ears with tiny white strokes.

color. The portion of the ear nearest the base should be the most vivid. As you reach the outside edges, add white and a small amount of black to the salmon color to dull it down to a warm grayish shade. Fill in the other ear with this gray color as well.

Use a small brush and burnt sienna to fill in the eye circle, then clean your brush and switch to white paint to highlight the eye by encircling it as shown.

Use the same brush to make your fawn's spots. I like to start with the spots that show just behind the head. These are small and slightly fan-shaped, running in two parallel rows along the fawn's spine to the tail. Feather the edges of the tail with long strokes.

The spots on the haunch need not be uniform in size or shape, but should conform to the direction the fur would naturally grow. Check the directional guide above and at right. Add spots to shadowed areas as well.

Use your white paint to outline both ears. Stroke in a line of white fur along the upper edge of your pink inner ear, longer at the base and growing shorter as you move back toward the tip.

To paint the fawn's white chest, prop up your stone at an angle. The fur at the chest should be delicate and fluffy.

Rendering the fur spots.

5 Fur Texture.

Now you are ready to give your stone animal its realistically furry texture. Mix white and gold to get a pale straw color and begin along the muzzle. Leave the center portion of the face (between the eyes and down the muzzle) brown, but angle a row of tiny, straw-colored fur lines just past the nose and around the bulge of the eye. Allow your strokes to grow longer as you move back along the curve of the forehead. On the lower side of the muzzle shingle in several sets of fur lines, filling in that portion of the face down to the jawline and all the way back to the white fur at the chest. Fan a set of strokes back from behind the eye as well. Give your fawn more expression by stroking in two sets of

The Art of Painting Animals on Rocks

eyebrow lines, angling them down and inward.

Use white paint to create the tuft of fur around the base of the outer ear. Then add highlights to the upper edge of that ear. Consult the directional guide as you fill in the head and throat.

Next, fill the entire haunch with overlapping fur lines, varying the length and direction of your strokes. At the point where the hind leg crooks, detail the lower leg with short, prickly lines. If you have a front leg showing, detail it in the same manner.

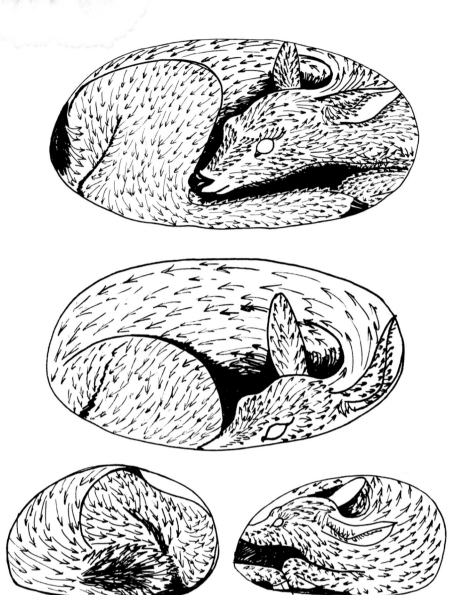

Follow this guide for realistic fur patches.

Texture the fur with rows of delicate lines.

Adding texture to haunch fur.

Detail the front leg with thin strokes.

How to Paint a Stone Fawn

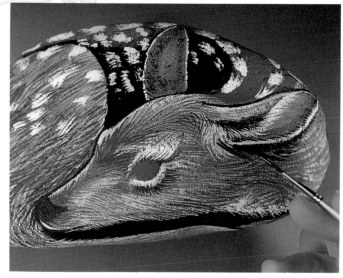

Emphasize the crook of the leg by intensifying the shadows around it.   Accent the ear by darkening the shadow under it.

6 Maximizing Contrast.

Mix a deep brown from black and burnt sienna. Add depth and enrich the texture of your fawn's fur by using this color to enhance the areas you just painted. Try to vary the length and direction of your strokes, but be sure to follow the same general fur direction. Emphasize the crook of the leg by darkening in a V-shaped area between the tail and the middle of the haunch.

This darker color can also be used to detail shadowed areas such as the center of the muzzle between the eyes. Run a series of short lines along the outside ear and just below the white highlighted area of the eye to add dimension.

To define each individual spot, stroke a series of short, dark lines around it. Darken the area directly below the nose and give the jawline added dimension by running a row of short, fine strokes along the bottom. Scatter darker fur lines along the hind leg, making your strokes denser toward the lower edge of the leg.

Don't neglect the spots along the back and in the midsection. They, too,

will stand out better with the addition of dark fur lines around their edges. Turn your fawn around and stroke a series of flowing lines along the curve of the spine. Finally, use this dark brown color to deepen the eye color, leaving only a narrow half-circle of lighter brown around the bottom.

With black paint and your smallest brush, outline the eye, then place an elongated oval-shaped iris horizontally

Dark outlines accent the spots.

Eye detail.

The Art of Painting Animals on Rocks

Check your fawn at different angles for incomplete areas.

in the upper center. Flick the tip of your brush along the upper edge of the eye to create delicate eyelashes. Use black sparingly to add contrast and definition anywhere else it may be needed. When you are satisfied with the quality and quantity of your fur lines, switch to white paint. Place a white dot in the upper section of the eye, and add a softer white gleam across the top of the nose. Sign and seal your finished piece, then look for the perfect place to display it. Try tucking your fawn among potted houseplants, or let him peer out from below your coffee table. Wherever you display him, he's certain to attract admiring attention.

Try tucking your finished creations among potted houseplants.

The Art of Painting Animals on Rocks

How to Paint
Fox Rocks

W ith their delicate, almost catlike faces and wonderful plumed tails, foxes are among the most exciting subjects for stone painting. I paint both red and gray foxes, but prefer the former because the crisp white ruff, muzzle and tail are so handsome against the warm reddish-orange tones of the coat.

Special care must be taken with the layout of foxes, however. The length of the muzzle can be distorted easily by the curve of the stone, rendering the whole face slightly cockeyed.

Foxes can be painted in just about any size, from kit foxes no bigger than tennis balls to larger-than-life versions. For this project your best bet lies somewhere between those extremes. A good fox rock should be plump and as close to round as possible, allowing ample room for those perky, upright ears. But the rock shouldn't be so round it won't sit firmly without tipping. Think in terms of a basketball with its bottom flattened.

The layout process will also be easier if you select a stone that has one slightly less convex side.

When you have a stone that fulfills these requirements, scrub it well and let it dry.

Look for the roundest stone you can find.

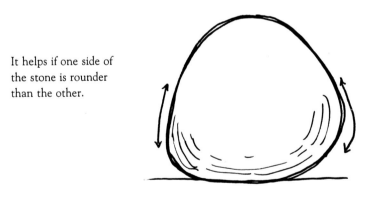

It helps if one side of the stone is rounder than the other.

What You'll Need

- black, red, white, gold and burnt sienna paint
- assorted brushes
- white chalk

A suitable fox rock.

1 The Basecoat.

Pour a large puddle of red paint into your dish and add small amounts of black until you get a deep burgundy shade (or you may buy acrylic paint in burgundy if you prefer). Use your largest brush to quickly cover all visible surfaces with this color. Allow the basecoat to dry thoroughly.

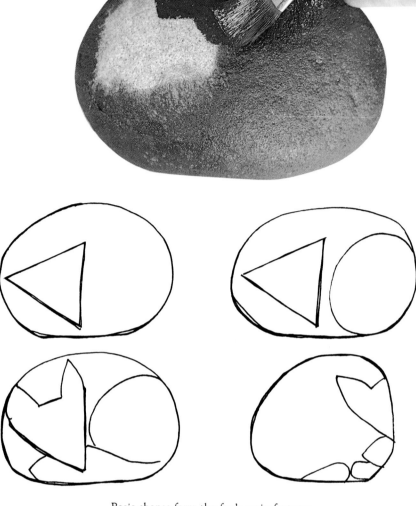

2 Layout.

Use chalk to sketch in the features and contours of your fox. Where a raccoon's face may be characterized by a heart shape, the fox's face begins with an equilateral triangle. The top section of the triangle should equal one-half the length of your stone as measured across from side to side. You can position the head horizontally, or tilt it at a 45-degree angle. Remember to leave plenty of room above it for the ears. If your head is too high on the stone, the ears may curve around the stone and disappear.

The bottom sides of the head triangle should come to a point just above the base of your stone. The haunch can be either a circle or an oval about the same width as the head. The tail curves up and rests beneath the snout. On some stones there may be room for the paws to show next to the tip of the tail.

Basic shapes form the fox's main features.

If so, make them two elongated ovals.

To lay out the face, bisect your triangle horizontally and then divide it in thirds vertically. Place the eyes at the two points where your horizontal line intersects the vertical lines. Foxes have

wide-set eyes. Space them between two and three eye-widths apart. The ears are also triangular. Use your vertical lines as guides. The total height of each ear should be roughly equivalent to one-half the length of the face

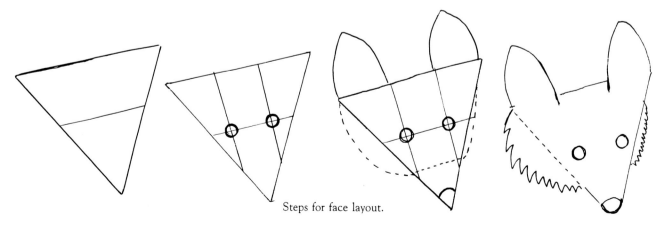

Steps for face layout.

82   *The Art of Painting Animals on Rocks*

Note how the proportion of the face ruff changes at different angles.

triangle. Indicate the ruff by adding a jagged line around the left side of the face. If your face is set at an angle, the other side of the face will require a much shallower curved line as the ruff will barely show. Indicate the nose by making a half-circle across the bottom of the face triangle. The nose should be just a bit larger than the diameter of an eye. Before going on, make sure your features are symmetrical. Hold a pencil or other straightedge even with the bottoms of the two eyes. The line between the eyes should be parallel to the one between the ears. Take the time to insure your features are properly aligned now to save disappointment with your finished piece.

Ready to paint.

3 Contours.

Establish your contours next, using black paint and a medium brush to outline the head, haunch and tail. Feather your brush strokes out and away from the top of the head until they extend just past the tips of the ears. Indicate shoulders by painting an M-shaped line behind the ears. Darken the areas around and between the head and haunch. Outline the eyes as shown, extending a line down from the lower inside corners. These lines should follow the tilt of the head. Blacken in the nose.

Eye shapes.

Outline the eyes and blacken the nose.

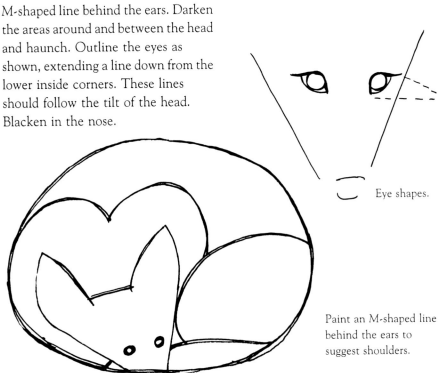

Paint an M-shaped line behind the ears to suggest shoulders.

How to Paint Fox Rocks

4 Building Contrast.

When your black shadows dry, switch to white paint. Fill in the tip of the tail. Then outline the muzzle, blunting the pointed end to round the nose. Paint both sides of the muzzle white, leaving the inside edge (the one next to the haunch) slightly thinner than the outside edge to account for the angle of the head. Leave the top along the length of the muzzle dark. Also leave a small gap of dark paint showing where the muzzle joins the bottom of the ruff.

Fan your strokes to fill out the ruff. The length of the ruff fur increases gradually as you move upward until it is even with the outside corner of the eye. On the other side the ruff can be indicated by stroking in a row of short curving white lines.

Outline the ears rather heavily with white and use your smallest brush to fill the insides of the ears with whiskers. Before moving on, place a faint line of white along the top of the nose to simulate a dull gleam.

Defining the ruff and ears.

5 Fur Texture.

Now mix equal parts of gold and white paint to get a pale straw color. Starting with the haunch, work all the way around the outside edge with a series of spiky fur lines. Next, fill in the entire haunch area. Overlap and cross your strokes in successive layers until you reach the top. Check the directional guides at left and below whenever you aren't sure how the fur should look.

Move to the face and add dimension to the muzzle by painting in a row of diagonal lines along either side, still leaving the narrow strip of dark paint down the center. Above the eyes, curve each stroke out like eyebrows. Shingle in several more sets to fill the

Follow directions for fur patches.

Fur patches from different angles.

The Art of Painting Animals on Rocks

Painting the haunch fur.

Overlap your fur lines for a sleek finish.

Leave a strip of base coat showing around the shoulders.

entire forehead area. Make a set of short, dense strokes between the ears so that the head stands out in strong contrast to the shadowy area behind it. Below the eyes, begin two more sets of lines at the inside corners at each side, leaving dark areas (like tear trails) untouched.

Turn your stone around and detail the shoulder areas. Begin your fur lines an inch or so beyond the black area between the ears. Fan your strokes out in overlapping rows until you reach the M-shaped outline of the shoulders. Skip over it, leaving a ½″ strip of the dark undercoat showing, then follow the contour of the shoulders with more sets of fur lines. As you reach the curved edge of the stone, leave one more swath of undercoat showing to add interest to the back of the stone. From there simply follow the curve of the stone all the way to the base along the back side. Fill out the tail with defining strokes along the top and bottom edges.

That completes the basic fur lines. Before going on, look your piece over for sufficient detail. This is a good time to heighten contrast where needed. Use your small brush and white paint to overlay another set of extremely fine fur lines along the inside curve of the haunch to make it stand out.

Longer strokes define the tail.

Feather light strokes up the snout into bushy eyebrows.

How to Paint Fox Rocks

85

6 Tinting.

Next mix several drops of burnt sienna with an equal amount of gold to get a warm red-brown. Fill in the eye circles with this color. Switching to your larger brush, add water to this reddish-brown color to make a wash. Test the consistency on newspaper to be sure the tint is transparent. Use this tint to deepen the color of select fur lines. Begin by feathering strokes out from behind the head, but leave the tips of your lines untinted. Move down to the next sets of lines on the back and tint the area closest to the shadowed borders, again leaving the tips untouched.

On the haunch, avoid tinting the outermost set of prickly strokes, but tint the inner fur lines. Remember, if the tint pigment is too heavy, it will obscure your original brush strokes. If that happens, pick up the excess pigment with a tissue while it is still wet and add more water to your wash.

On the face, tint the area between the eyes and feather your strokes into the forehead. Leave the light areas around the eyes. Tint the entire tail.

Filling in the eyes.

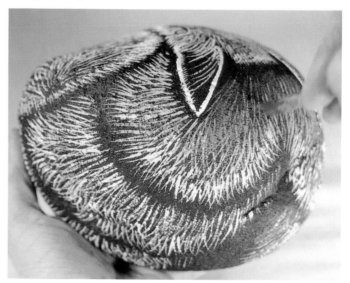

Tinting behind the ears.

Avoid coloring the edges of the haunch.

The Art of Painting Animals on Rocks

Make sure tinting wash isn't opaque or it will hide fur lines.

Tinting the bushy tail.

7 Fur Details.

Now mix burnt sienna with enough black to get a deep brown. This color will add the finishing touch to the texture of your fox's coat. Use your small brush to scatter dark fur lines among the lighter ones on the fox's haunch. The lines should be denser around the bottom half of the haunch and more sparing along the upper half. Add some dark fur to the face for visual interest and contrast.

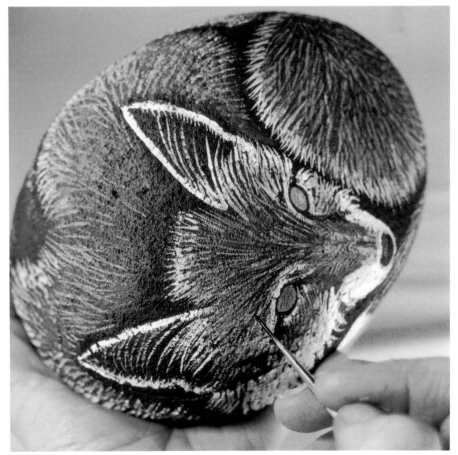

Detailing the face.

Accent the haunch with delicate dark lines.

How to Paint Fox Rocks

8 Finishing Touches.

Clean your brush and use straight black to paint the irises in the eyes. Outline the eyes so they are crisp and clean. Use the black to enhance the definition between the muzzle and ruff. With the point of your brush, stipple several rows of follicles across the muzzle and add four or five curving black whiskers.

To give the eyes more depth, mix a touch of sienna to the black on your brush to get a deep brown. Encircle the top half of each eye. Add a dot of pure white to the top of each iris to make the eye look wet.

Finishing the eyes.

Whisker detail.

Add sparkle to the eyes with tiny white dots.

The Art of Painting Animals on Rocks

A frequently overlooked area on all stone animals is the side just below the head. Turn your stone to that side and add fur lines if needed. To finish, use medium gray to outline and define the black paws.

As I mentioned earlier, foxes can be done in a variety of sizes. Kit foxes make nice paper weights. Look for good photographs to use for reference.

Be sure not to overlook the side below the head.

Try different sizes. Kit foxes make great paperweights.

The Art of Painting Animals on Rocks

How to Paint
Stoney Owls

Birds present a completely different kind of challenge for the stone painter. Downy fluff and smooth overlapping feathers replace fine fur lines. As a rule, there is little or no contouring involved. But not all birds are good subjects. Many simply are not compact enough to fit neatly onto common rock shapes. Owls, however, are particularly well suited for stone painting. Their bodies are basic, uncomplicated forms that adapt easily to many different stone shapes. The owls I paint most often are called sawwhets. While they aren't as dramatically patterned as some owl species, they do offer nice contrasts between breast, back and wings, and they have wonderful little faces.

In your search for a possible owl stone, look for a flat-bottomed, wide-based upright stone. It should taper gently to a rounded top. An owl stone might be symmetrical, it might tilt to one side, or even lean forward, so long as it will sit without tipping over.

Tilted stones work fine, provided they don't tip over easily.

What You'll Need

- white, black, gold, yellow and burnt sienna acrylic paints
- assorted brushes
- a pencil
- measuring tape
- chalk

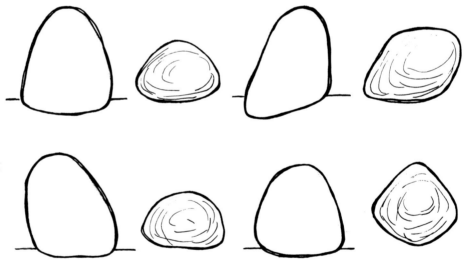

Suitable stone shapes.

A perfect owl rock.

Choosing a suitable site for the face is the most important layout factor for your owl. The face area should be a relatively wide, flat plane. If the stone has an outward curve, the widest point should form the vertical midpoint of the face. After you have selected the site for the face, determine the best place for the tail. Unlike most animals, owls can turn their heads in nearly any direction, so the tail need not be directly behind or to one side of the head. If the stone you've chosen has a bump at the base, this would be the logical spot for the tail, regardless of where it is in relation to the face. In fact, some of the most successful owl stones are those where the owl is peering back over his shoulder.

Your owl could stand up quite tall, or it might be lower and wider, as though hunkered down.

Once you have a rock you think will work, scrub it well and let it dry. Then, using your largest brush, cover all exposed surfaces with white paint.

A snowy white base coat.

A variety of owl poses.

1 Layout.

When this base coat is dry, measure the stone's height. This measurement will help you determine the dimensions for the face. For stones 8″ or taller, the face may go halfway down the rock and nearly all the way across. On smaller stones, though, the owl will look best when the face is slightly shorter. To illustrate these proportions, I measured a number of my recent stone owls, and came up with the following figures, which may be helpful:

Owl #1
• Overall height—7″
• Vertical face measurement—3″
• Horizontal face measurement—4½″

Owl #2
• Overall height—6″
• Vertical face measurement—2½″
• Horizontal face measurement 4″

Owl #3
• Overall height—5½″
• Vertical face measurement—2″
• Horizontal face measurement—3¾″

Some variance is possible due to the shape of your stone, but it's safe to say your basic layout won't be too far off if you keep these relationships in mind. Use a pencil to measure off the proportions for your face oval.

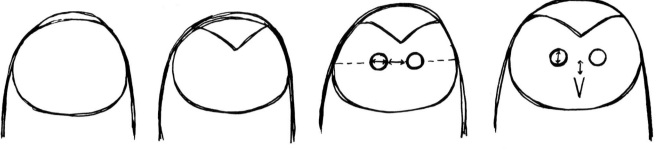

Steps for face layout.

After the face oval is in place, modify it by creating a V-shape in the middle of the forehead. Then bisect the oval horizontally and use the midline as a guide for the eyes. Owls have dramatically large, round eyes. Eye diameter will vary with the size of your stone. On the three owls I measured previously, the size of the eyes are:

- 8″ tall owl—just over ⅝″ across
- 7″ tall owl—½″ across
- 6″ tall owl—just over ⅜″ across
- 5½″ tall owl—just under ⅜″ across

Use the height of your own stone to determine the size of the eyes, then center them on the midline one eye space apart. To determine beak placement, measure one eye-width down from between the eyes on the midline. Mark that as the top of the beak. The beak itself should be a narrow triangle whose point doesn't quite reach to the bottom of the face.

Now turn your rock so the back is facing you. Draw a neck line around the back of the head. Indicate the tail with a wide V at the base. The sides of this V should bow gently outward around the curving sides of your stone and touch the perimeters of the face oval in front. If you look at your rock sideways, the wing lines should cut diagonally from the face to the tail. The remaining portion of the body will be the breast.

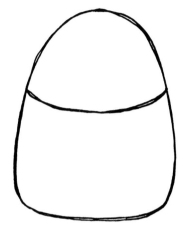

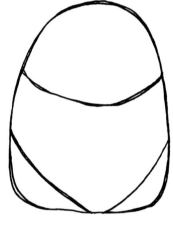

Vertical measurement may be up to 50 percent of overall height.

Horizontal measurement may be up to 75 percent of overall height.

Overall height.

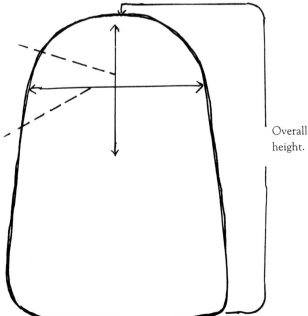

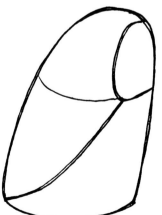

Blocking in the wing and tail areas.

2 Face and Head Details.

Use your narrow brush to outline the eye circles in black. Paint the beak next, making the point sharp and well defined. The wide upper end should be ragged-looking to create the illusion of small overlapping feathers. Next use a medium flat brush to encircle the face with short, dense strokes. Create feathery points along the bottom of the face. Fill in the rest of the head shape with solid black all the way around. Let the paint dry.

Now take up your finest brush and switch to gold paint softened with a little white. Use this color to make thin, dense lines like sunrays emanating from the eyes and beak. Leave a border of white encircling the eyes, but allow your brushstrokes to overlap some of the dark areas on the head. Use gold at full strength to fill in the eye circles. The owl's eyes will be the focal point of the piece, so take your time to paint them as neat and round as you can. If you accidently paint over your black outlines, retrace them in black later when the eyes are dry.

Shade the back of the head.

Subtle gold highlights surround the eyes and beak.

Outline with bold black strokes.

Gold eye color.

The Art of Painting Animals on Rocks

3 Feather Patterns.

To feather the breast, use a medium, round bristled brush and burnt sienna. Your brushstrokes can be random. Begin with a raggedy-looking row of feathers below the black edging at the neck. Next make several vertical rows of broken strokes down the breast. Allow these strokes to vary in both size and spacing, but curve them slightly inward. Leave plenty of white area showing between these strokes.

Tilt your stone backward to expose the lower front edge and brush a series of dense, random lines to shadow the bottom portion of the breast. Use a brush that will allow you to taper your strokes.

Next use your larger brush to mix black and burnt sienna into a deep brown. Turn your stone so the back is facing you and fill in the back and tail feathers. Leave a narrow collar of white showing between the head and shoulders.

Roughing in the breast feathers.

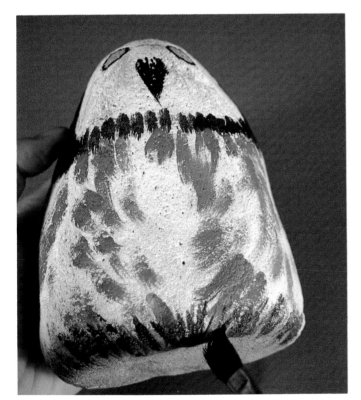

Tilt your stone to paint the base feathers.

Back and tail feathers.

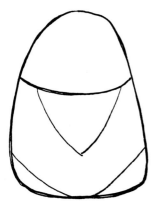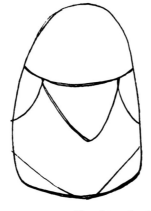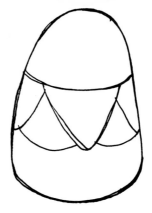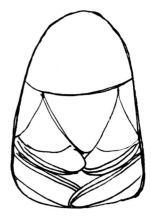

Sketching the feather pattern.

4 **Wing and Tail Feather Layout.**
Once the back is dry, use chalk to sketch the pattern for the feathers.

Begin at the neck and extend a *V* shape halfway down the back, mirroring the *V* of the tail. On each side make narrower *V* shapes like epaulettes at the shoulders. Connect the bottom points of these *V* shapes with curved lines. Below these curved lines, sketch in two sets of overlapping feather patches as shown. If you are dissatisfied with your layout, rub out the chalk and revise.

Feathers meet to form *V* shapes.

Feather design.

5 **Painting the Feathers.**
When you're satisfied with the layout, add a series of white strokes along the back *V* with a small or medium brush. Use your narrower brush to outline both upper and lower sets of wing feathers, and make a series of white dots along the two curving lines connecting the shoulders to the back *V*.

Next, mix burnt sienna and gold paint in equal proportions to get a warm golden-brown. With your narrow brush make a row of connected *U* shapes along the white neckline in back. Do a second row below the first, starting each *U* in the middle of the one above so that you have an overlapping effect. You should have room for four or more rows, each one shorter than the one above until there is space

Outline the tail feathers with a liner brush.

U shapes overlap at the neck.

for only a single *U* at the point. Do a similar pattern on the epaulettes at each shoulder.

To connect the shoulder pattern and the back pattern, make a series of diagonal feather lines as shown. Add depth and visual interest to the very bottom set of wing feathers by running

several thin lines of brown alongside the white outlines.

Add black to the brown color you've been using and shade the bottom edges of each scalloped row of *U*-shaped feathers. Use this same color to shadow the base with thin, wispy brushstrokes.

The Art of Painting Animals on Rocks

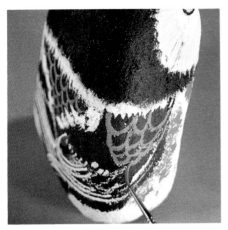

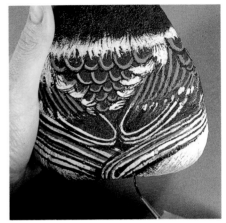

Paint a series of overlapping *U* shapes at each shoulder.

Diagonal feather lines connect the wings to the back.

Delicate brown lines are interspersed with white among the tail feathers.

6 Head Feathers.

Going back to the head, use a clean, narrow brush and white paint to begin a series of short, crooked, broken lines starting along the top border of the face and radiating back into the black area of the head. Allow your strokes to become more uniform as you work around the sides of the head. The strokes should radiate out like short spokes. Add consecutive layers of similar strokes to cover the back and sides of the head.

White wavy lines radiate from the top of the head.

Continue layering white lines . . .

. . . down the back of the head.

7 Feather Details.

Switch back to the deep brown shade and add crisp details to the lighter brown feathers at the breast. Paint a row of dense, random strokes just below the neckline. Then scatter more of these lines in clustered sets among the breast feathers.

Detail the breast area with random fine lines.

8 Finishing Details.

Surround the eyes with delicate lashlike strokes. At the inside lower corner of each eye, elongate the strokes and fan them out to look particularly dense and heavy. Allow a few strokes to reach into the top of the beak and a few more to stretch horizontally above the beak from either side until they almost touch.

Fan another set of strokes below each eye. A few should even overlap the top of the beak, while others curve away in the opposite direction.

Brush in a set of short lines just inside the face oval from either side of the V. Follow the curve of the face. Refer to the directional guide for feather placement.

Fill in the eyes with black, oval irises. The irises should be slightly skewed toward the center of each eye circle. Darken the upper portion of each eye with burnt sienna to add depth. Then highlight the eye by stroking a narrow half-circle of bright yellow paint around the lower half.

Finally, switch to white paint and define any light areas that may require more detail with your narrow brush. Pay particular attention to the outer edges of the wings on either side of the breast. These feathers should look fluffy.

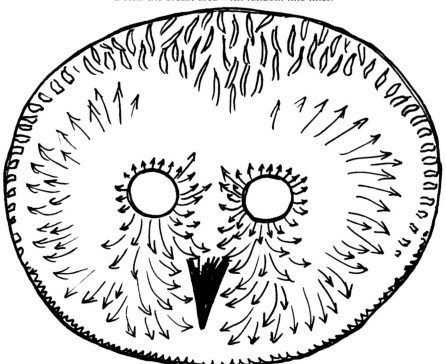

Follow the arrows for facial feather patterns.

Face detail.

Irises should be slightly skewed toward the center.

The Art of Painting Animals on Rocks

You may also want to add some white strokes to the breast, overlapping the brown streaks here and there. Finish by placing two small dots in the inside upper quadrant of each eye for a lifelike sparkle.

Owls are quite ornamental and will add an exciting touch to any decor. Try perching one or two on a section of wood for an almost sculptural effect.

Touching up the wing edges.

A white glimmer sparkles in each piercing eye.

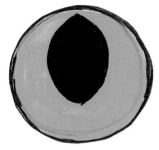

Steps for eye detail.

The Art of Painting Animals on Rocks

Expand Your Horizons
A Gallery of
Stone Animals

The previous chapters have shown you how to create a number of different stone animals step-by-step. Once you have mastered the basic techniques there is no end to the variations. These next few pages are intended to give you just a taste of other possibilities.

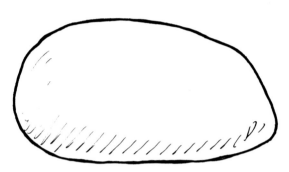

Colt

Like fawns, colts are characterized by the way their long legs fold beneath them. Look for a fawn-type stone, one with a "crook" at one end to accommodate the angle of the back leg. The colt's head is longer than a fawn's, the muzzle more rounded, and the ears slightly shorter.

Colt stone and layout.

A colt nestled in the hay.

Wild Cats

The leopard and cheetah are two wild cats that make arresting subjects. Note the way a lump on the leopard stone was transformed into a shoulder blade. Wild cats may be handled much like domestic cats, but are most effective in crouching rather than curled positions. Other wild cats to try are tigers, lions cougars and bobcats. Photographs of these animals will help you envision how they might fit onto stones.

Here's my leopard curled up on the hearth at home.

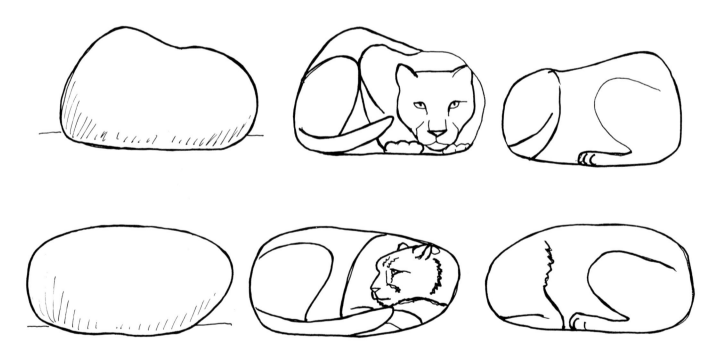

Stone shapes and layout for wildcats.

The Art of Painting Animals on Rocks

Cheetah (front).

Cheetah (rear).

Leopard (front).

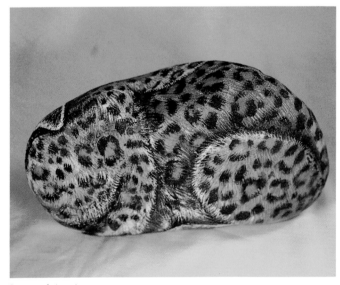

Leopard (rear).

A Gallery of Stone Animals

Mouse

Good mouse stones aren't always easy to find, but if you come across one, these little rodents can be fun to paint. Look for a pear-shaped stone. It should be similar to that for a rock rabbit, but more pointed at the end and preferably a little flatter overall. In coloring and execution this project is also similar to the rabbit, the differences being primarily the short, more rounded ears and larger, bulgy, closely set black eyes. The tail can be painted in as though wrapped around one side, or you can glue on a length of rawhide lacing.

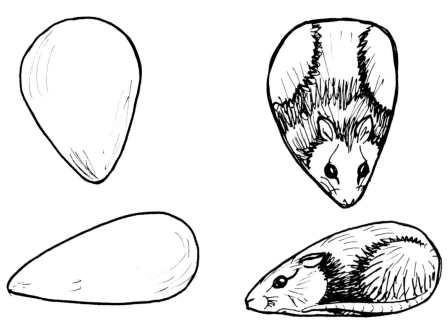

Mouse rocks and layout.

A very cautious mouse.

The Art of Painting Animals on Rocks

Pandas

These roly-poly critters create real "panda-monium" among animal lovers and are surprisingly easy to paint. Look for a plump "tombstone"-shaped rock. The top in particular needs to be broad and well rounded for best results. The panda is basically black and white, with dark brown for the eyes and a touch of gold mixed with gray to detail its white fur for softer, more subtle shading.

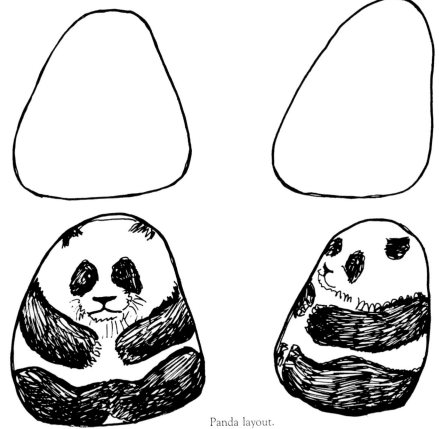

Panda layout.

Side.

Rear.

Front.

A Gallery of Stone Animals

Dog

This little fellow seems to be imploring someone to give him a treat. I used an upright stone with a pronounced forward tilt. Small, long-haired dogs can be handled like long-haired cats in a crouched position.

Side.

Front.

Rear.

Stone shapes and layout choices for long-haired dogs.

The Art of Painting Animals on Rocks

Beavers

Like raccoons, beavers can be done in two basic poses, either crouching or standing upright with the paws tucked under the chin. I cut leaf-shaped tails from a sheet of scrap leather and darken them with a light coat of black spray paint in a matt finish. Leave extra length on the tail so the base can be glued to the bottom of the stone. Although a beaver's teeth are not always visible in photographs, I invariably paint them in as people seem disappointed when that distinctive trademark is not apparent.

Various beaver projects.

Double Animals

A number of double animals fit nicely on rounded stones of assorted sizes. While foxes with kits may be "too cute" for your taste, others are charmed by the combination of mother and baby. The fox layout is in the same fashion as a single animal, then the kit is added, usually tucked behind the tail. The same thing can be done with a mother raccoon and her kit. Make sure your babies look like babies, though, and not simply like miniature versions of adults. Usually this means giving them shorter muzzles and ears, and larger eyes.

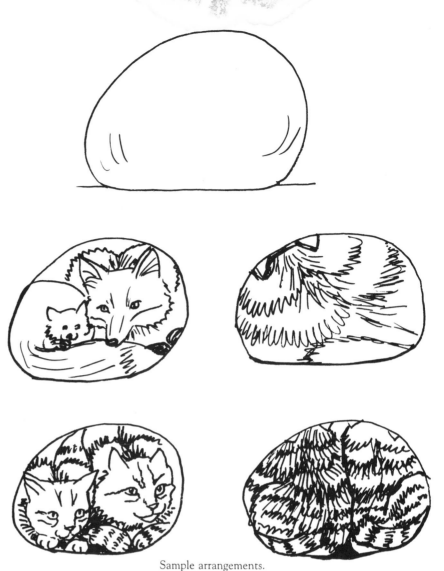

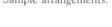

Sample arrangements.

The Art of Painting Animals on Rocks

Doubles can be twins or mother-baby combinations.

Double cats and kittens. Not only are these fun to do, they can be done on a wide range of rock shapes. You can make identical twins by painting the same animal twice, or vary the position, expression and coloration for an even more dramatic look. Double cats can also be done with one facing forward and the other facing backward.

Double squirrels. I have painted these baby squirrels a number of times since coming across a photograph that helped me see how I could fit them onto a stone. Ordinarily squirrels are difficult subjects because their fluffy tails do not readily conform to stone shapes. But these two, clinging to one another with their tails wrapped around their feet, are made to order for painting on stone.

Approach them much as you would wild bunnies, beginning with a black base coat. Note that squirrels' front paws have very distinctive fingers.

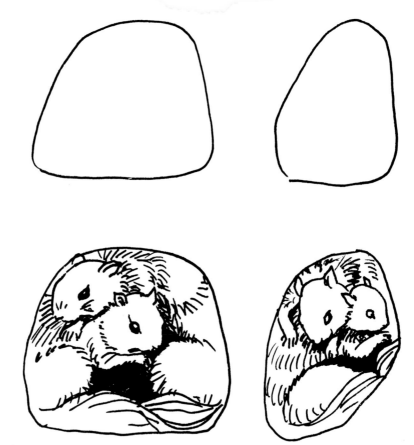

Sample arrangements.

The Art of Painting Animals on Rocks

Paired squirrels (back).

Paired squirrels (side).

Pebble Pets

There is something irresistible about miniature animals. If you enjoy doing very fine detail, these can be a lot of fun. Kids in particular seem to enjoy working on such a small scale. Be sure to select smooth stones for best effect.

Any animal in this book can be done in a "pebble pet" version with a bit of patience. They come in handy as small gift items and usually sell as fast as I can make them.

Other animals I have painted over the years include calves, wolves, brown bears, cocker spaniel, chow chow and German shepherd dogs, and even a ferret. Trying new animals keeps stone painting fresh and exciting. I am always looking for new challenges. That's one more reason why stone painting can be such a satisfying creative outlet.

A potpourri of pebble pets.

The Art of Painting Animals on Rocks

Display your rock animals in the house . . .

. . . on the porch . . .

Enhancing Your Decor With Rock Animals

Your rock animals can be displayed anywhere in your living space. They can add various moods to your room, from cute and cozy to dramatic and exotic. Use your imagination to display each unique and beautiful conversation piece. My rock animals have made their home in every room in, and out of, our house—even the barn.

. . . even in the barn!

Marketing Tips

I hope the projects in this book have inspired you to keep painting stones, refining your techniques and developing your own special style. With time you are likely to see even more possibilities than I have shown you. Friends and relatives may come to treasure your stone creations as gifts at Christmas and birthdays as mine have. If you find yourself thoroughly hooked on stone painting, you might begin to wonder if the quality of your work is good enough to sell.

Displaying your work. One way to find out is to participate in an arts and crafts fair. Choose an event where booth space is relatively inexpensive. Plan ahead and make sure you have enough inventory to make the venture worthwhile. Put some thought into how best to display your pieces. Polished slabs of hardwood make attractive bases for larger works and will give them a "sculptural" appearance. Cats can be nestled on pillows or into inexpensive baskets, but be sure to figure the cost of the pillow or basket in your sales price. Many people will expect to get them as part of the package. Sections of logs make rustic pedestals for wildlife stones like raccoons, while a simple bed of straw can set off a fawn rock in an appealing way.

Pricing. Pricing your work will probably be a matter of trial and error. Beginners may start by keeping prices low, say under ten dollars on smaller pieces, to encourage those oh-so-inspiring first sales. As skill level increases, the prices your work commands will naturally rise. If your stones sell briskly, that is evidence the price is too low and could be raised. Another school of thought, however, is that an artist should begin with a higher price and adjust it gradually downward until it seems acceptable to a reasonable

number of customers.

Building a business. Once you have established that there is a market for your painted stones, it's a good idea to print some business cards to pass out. As you become more proficient, you will almost certainly be asked about commissions. Cat owners, in particular, are apt to want their pet's likeness captured on stone. Insist on receiving good photos of the subject, and agree on a price at the outset to avoid any misunderstandings. Dog lovers may also inquire about stone portraits of their pets. Due to the tremendous differences between breeds, dogs can be trickier than cats, but if you are comfortable with the challenge, give it a try. You can always forfeit the commissions if you find yourself unable to do justice to the project. Short-haired dogs are somewhat similar to fawns,

while long-haired dogs can be handled more in the manner of Persian cats or foxes. I rarely do dogs unless it is by commission because people who love dogs usually have a favorite breed, while cat lovers tend to be less particular. And I always offer a money-back guarantee on commissioned work to insure satisfaction.

By distributing your cards and displaying your work at various fairs and shows, you should be able to build up business in custom work and special orders, particularly around the holidays.

When experience has given you an idea of how much you can realistically charge, the next step may be to market your stones through retail outlets. Shop owners on the lookout for unusual items might inquire about a wholesale pricelist. Remember most

Sample business card.

retailers expect to double the price of anything they buy. Ask yourself, based on personal experience, what kind of wholesale pricing would give you a satisfactory return on your time and talent. You don't want to price your work out of the range most people are willing to pay. If you are a prolific painter as I am, wholesale accounts can expand your markets and keep you busy. But if you enjoy taking your time with each stone you paint and don't want to be pressured to produce quickly, wholesaling is probably not for you.

Another possibility is selling on commission. Since this requires a certain level of trust, stick to well-established businesses. The standard agreement for selling on commission is that you set the price for your work and the shop owner keeps a portion of the sales price of each item sold, usually be-

tween 30 and 40 percent. The advantage of this type of arrangement is that you will make more than you might be able to charge wholesale while keeping the actual sales price lower. On the down side, you won't get paid until a piece sells. Commission also means more bookkeeping for you. It's important to keep careful records of which items you have placed in what stores. Most shopkeepers are honest and pay within thirty days on any sales they make. But nearly everyone who has sold work on commission can tell stories of waiting months for payment, or of having unscrupulous merchants close down and disappear, taking their ill-gotten inventory along. So it pays to be discriminating in your choice of outlets. Look for stores that specialize in handcrafted items, or upscale gift shops that appreciate the value of your

unique, one-of-a-kind work. Better still are galleries whose clientele will see your stones as works of art rather than mere crafts. My best outlet by far is a wildlife art gallery where my work commands a respectable price and turnover is dependably steady.

Yet another option is to see if your area has a craft mall where booth space is rented by the month and sales are handled by staff salespeople. You will be charged a commission on any items that sell, but unlike other outlets, you can set up your own sales area. An attractive display and realistic prices could make this a lucrative venture.

Whether you choose to produce in volume or confine your efforts to "limited editions" for friends and family, stone painting can be a terrific low-cost hobby and a truly satisfying outlet for your creative urge.

Author, Lin Wellford, on her porch with part of her stone menagerie.

The Art of Painting Animals on Rocks

Index